BOYS TO MEN

THE LOST ART OF THE RITE OF PASSAGE

Boys to Men
The Lost Art of the Rite of Passage
Allen Jones

Cover Design by Dallas Drotz and Drotz Design
Illustrations by Dallas Drotz and Drotz Design

Printed by Data Reproductions Corporation
Printed in the Unites States of America
First printing 2012

Published by:
AJ Communications
12636 195th Ave Ct E
Bonney Lake, WA 98391-6067
www.allenjones.org

ISBN 978-0-9881740-0-9

DEDICATION

For every man who has a son,

Who has a dream for his son,

Who desires to see his son become a better man than he,

Welcome to the club!

This book is for you and all those like you,

Of which I am one.

We can make a difference!

PRAISE FOR BOYS TO MEN

Allen Jones is a consummate leader with passion for developing leaders of all ages. His business savvy and street smarts are only surpassed by his incredible heart to worship his God. Allen has positioned himself as more than qualified to speak to the subject of boys transitioning to manhood. I would wholeheartedly encourage not only every father, but also every parent to read his thoughts in this powerful work of art and love.

Roger Archer
Senior Pastor
Foursquare Puyallup Church
And author of *The Leadership Lock*

CONTENTS

PREFACE

I'd like to tell you about a man I know. I have found that a little contrast is always helpful in providing context. I'd like to introduce you to my friend and mentor Norman (Norm) Lee. A little history might be helpful here. I met Mr. and Mrs. Lee, whom I affectionately refer to as Mom and Dad, in the fall of 1980. I had met their youngest son, Steve, at high school and we quickly became very good friends, best friends. Steve passed away several years later in a tragic accident. However, the relationship that started with that friendship has endured over 30 years later with Mom and Dad.

I have known Mom and Dad Lee for a long time, and they have both contributed so much to my life in ways I do not have the space to articulate. Mom is one of the most significant women in my life. What she taught me about grace, kindness, love, patience, forgiveness, and faithfulness are in and of themselves invaluable. This space, however, is primarily about Mr. Lee's influence.

I didn't fully realize how much influence Dad had on my life as I was writing this book. I had originally included a bit of his story in Chapter 11, Money (It's still there). While wrapping up the book, I mailed him the excerpt that contained his information, and asked him to review it and provide any corrections. He called me back from Arizona where they winter; he asked if we could meet when he got home to Washington, instead of doing a simple phone call. I recall at the moment I just wanted to get this book done. But I have such great respect and regard for Mr. Lee, that the only thing I would ever say to him is, "Yes, sir." And I did.

When they returned home from Arizona, Dad called me, and we sat down and talked. I was expecting a quick meeting to make sure I had my information correct. But something very profound unfolded before me that quite honestly came as a surprise, something I hadn't anticipated when I scheduled that time to sit with him for a little fact checking.

Today, Dad is 83 years old, but you would not know it from seeing him or spending time with him. He is vibrant and has great energy; he's active playing golf, and working on his commercial properties and his residences when he's in town.

He gave me some of that energy that evening as we sat down together. As one minute rolled into the next, one story into the next, as he put his life into order for me, I slowly began to realize just how much he has influenced me. I had heard so many of these stories in little snippets over 30 years, but I had not fully realized their cumulative effect. His finger prints are all over this book as they are all over my life.

Dad's life and his reflections, his lessons, his wisdom, and experiences are simple and yet profound. He was born just prior to the Great Depression. He lived through World War II, the Korean War, the Vietnam War, multiple stock market crashes, and 9/11; he has experienced significant personal losses, and much, much more. He has seen a lot, and lived through a lot. He is also a very wealthy man financially, and more importantly, very wealthy in the love and adoration of family and friends. He has a story to tell, and that is maybe another book.

As I sat with him at my ripe old age of 47, I was humbled at what an enormous gift I had been given. Then, of course, I had a moment of remorse as I realized so much had been squandered in my youth. Have you ever been there? As I consider all that I have learned and come to believe to be true about what comprises the enduring qualities of an authentic man, I realize that I had a living example right in front of me. I had formed my "definition of a real man" long before I interviewed Dad; I am now more convinced than ever that it is a great definition. You will feel his influence in nearly every single chapter of this book, in the way he lived his life out before me:

Character and integrity – he is always consistent, always trustworthy, the most authentic man I know.

Values and goals – it is always obvious what matters to him in where he spends his time and money, and the focus he maintains to achieve his goals, never distracted.

Chivalry – in the way I have always seen him care for, provide for, and protect Mom.

Sexual integrity – he is a faithful and committed man to one woman, and has only known one woman.

People – his entire life is characterized by his authentic love for people. His success in life is marked by being genuinely likeable, and his adroit skill in engendering people's high regard.

Money – it's chronicled in that specific chapter.

Work – I saw a man whose quality of life is attributable, in large part, to his personal ethos – if you wanted to get ahead, be the best man on the job, no matter what the job was, and when you do something, you give your all.

Faith – he comes from a generation that doesn't talk much about personal things, and faith is one of them. But I have seen his faith in God color every action, every personal philosophy, and every tragedy and triumph of his life.

As I was leaving the house to go visit Mr. Lee, my son Brendan asked where I was going; I told him. He asked me, "Dad, are Grammy and Poppy (as they are affectionately referred to by grandkids) rich"? I said, "Yes." He then commented, "You would never know it by being around them, Dad." And that may be the most impressive statement of all.

The point of this is not simply about a mentor. The point of this is to contemplate how we may have lost our way as men, and project forward to what we may be able to regain: the enduring qualities that produce a real, authentic, durable man, the kind of man the world so desperately needs. I will simply close with this quote from C.S. Lewis:

> *We all want progress, but if you're on the wrong road,*
> *progress means doing an about-turn and walking back*
> *to the right road; in that case, the man who turns back*
> *soonest is the most progressive.*

Thank you, Dad, for sharing and allowing me to share.

ACKNOWLEDGEMENTS

This book would not have come into being if not for the patience, grace, and feedback of my wife, Donna. She also played the role of "cheerleader" for this vulnerable male ego.

Without question, my sons, Devan and Brendan, are the inspiration for this book. Boys to Men would not exist if they did not exist. They were the guinea pigs for this process, and together we learned a ton. The time with my boys is one of my most prized possessions in life.

My beautiful daughter, ClaraAnn, is a nearly equal inspiration. She will be someone's wife one day, and she was always in my mind as I thought, "What kind of man do I want my daughter to find?"

This book is credible, in part, because of my experiences. I wish to thank my parents, Robert (Bob) Jones and Sally Inman, who, for the cause of helping fathers raise great men, had to be vulnerable, permitting me to "go inside" my family while I was growing up.

I must acknowledge the awesome men in my life that encouraged me, mentored me, participated in my boys' Rites of Passage, and provided valuable input to this work: Randy Dunn, Tony Burke, Doily Fulcher, Eric Boles, Dick Anderson, Jim Edinger, Roger Archer, Rick Metzger, Paul Gast, Thomas Beckworth, Dean Horstman, and Lee (and Kathleen) Britt.

Finally, to the men who have faithfully written and shared their experiences in an innumerable number of books that I have read since 1997 on how to be a man and how to properly raise one. I cannot begin to recount them by name; you would recognize many of these authors. You'll find their work in the bibliography. No person arrives at a place, as I have in writing this book, alone. I owe much to those who, through pen to paper, put their passion down in ink and shared it with the world – my boys and I thank you, and so do the men who read this book and are helped by it.

In addition to those acknowledged thus far, I would like to take a moment and make mention of a few people who, in the process of putting this work together, made personal contributions that allowed Boys to Men to come to fruition. I am enormously grateful for all who gave in support of this project, and to these few people, I give the title of Visionary Founder to this project, because they believe so strongly in the cause of raising great men, and they see this work as a solution:

Mark Hunter

Jeff and Aimee Wilkins

Bob and Ann Jones

Tye and Anita Bratvold

John F. Kelley

Thank you!

THE DEFINITION OF A REAL MAN

Strong in character and tender in nature; courageous at heart and compassionate in deed; gentle in speech, but confident in action; meek in his attitude, but tenacious in his convictions; he lives life fully, but selflessly, putting himself second to all things important; he loves his wife second only to his God; he will lay his life down for his family and friends, this man leaves no one behind. He lives with a purpose larger than his life; he is a values-driven man whose name is beyond reproach, he is known for his integrity; his wife adores him; his kids honor and respect him; his friends trust and admire him.

He is a man of his word.

INTRODUCTION

AN EAGLE'S LIFE

By nature, bald eagle parents are very intentional in the development of their young, the eaglet. There is a season when the eagles are young and their parents keep them warm and dry, feed them, and literally keep them under their wings. Once the young eagles reach a certain stage of maturity and have gotten all their feathers, the parents begin to stir up the nest by tossing out the soft nesting material that had kept the baby eagles comfortable. Because the young eagles are now less comfortable, they are forced to stand on their own two feet. This strengthens their legs, muscles, and talons. At a certain stage of their development, the parents begin to reduce, almost to the point of stopping, the feeding of the eaglets. They do this to make the little ones even more uncomfortable and force them to take the necessary next steps to maturity. This includes the ultimate goals of flight, feeding themselves, starting their own lives, finding their own mates, and independence. They understand that if the young eagles are coddled and made too comfortable, they will not do anything on their own.

When young eagles are old enough to fly, they do not realize they have this capability. In fact, they are still terrified of falling out of the nest as they begin to flirt with the edge out of desperation and necessity. The adult parents of these eaglets know the time has come for these young ones to fly, so they begin to entice them out of the nest by flying by with food in their beaks, close enough for the now-ravenous young eagles to see and smell the food they long for.

The day inevitably comes when the eaglets, after experimenting with a little wing flapping, and a couple of daring jumps close to the edge of the nest, must take the plunge. As dangerous as this situation is, it's for their own good if they are to become adult eagles. The young eagles, having never been flight tested, sit at the edge of the nest, knowing they have to fly at some point, but are afraid of falling to their death. The eaglets flutter, jump and finally get into the air for a few moments, not going more than just a few feet from the safety of the nest. Then they come back down to the edge of the nest. They may do this several times until they have enough courage to take the final plunge out of the nest and into the air. The young eagles do not have a choice; they must learn to fly or they will die.

An old myth is that if the eagle is unsuccessful in its flight attempt, before it hits the ground and dies, its father swoops down and picks it up. Not true. This is a romantic notion that makes us feel good, but the truth is, 40% of eagles don't survive their first flight attempt.

While this seems harsh, remember that by nature the eagle parents have the best interest of the eaglets at the center of their activity. However, best intentions don't necessarily produce great results. The young eagles must learn to stand before they can fly, and fly in order to be independent and self-sufficient. If they aren't ready to leave the nest when they finally do, they die nearly half the time.

We have the privilege of observing the eagle, of extrapolating incredible illustrations, parallels, and lessons for ourselves. For example, we see teamwork seldom seen by human parents. The parents work in tandem to prepare their young eagle. They aren't fighting with each other about what they should or shouldn't do depending on how well or poorly they were parented, bringing their own biases into their parenting. We see the intentional nurturing to prepare the young eagle for departure from the nest. The eagle parents know what their job is; it's hardwired into them.

Their purpose is clear: raise their young eagles to leave and live their own lives. Period.

We also see something very striking that reveals another aspect of our current culture in America. Forty percent of those young eagles that leave the nest fail; they die. Right now, I suspect that at least 40%, and depending on how you define "fail," a far greater number than 40% of our young men are failing and dying, both literally and figuratively.

This is where the analogy ends. We are not simply animals. The eagle doesn't have a choice in the matter; it is driven by instinct. It does what it does because it has to. As humans, we get the enormous privilege of choice, or free will. However, there is another side to the coin of privilege – responsibility. All too often as humans, and specifically to this book, parents, and even more to the point, fathers, we enjoy the privilege, but don't accept the responsibility.

Two remarkable things occurred to me as I studied this fascinating animal. One, we fail to understand and employ the great lessons of the bald eagle in how it prepares its young eagle to leave the nest. And two, we then emulate the bald eagle when 40% or more of our young men in our society fail and die. The eagle doesn't have a choice in this outcome. We do.

MY LIFE

As you grew up as a boy and a son, did your life have the thoughtful, intentional, mature, focused, accountable, and developmental environment as provided in the illustration above? Mine did not. The result was the same in my life as it is for 40% of the young eagles. In interacting closely with many men over the last 15 years, first as a business consultant, helping people become more personally effective, and getting to know them through that process, and later as a pastor interacting, counseling, and living life with a lot of men, I believe that my experience is typical. And tragically, my experience was better than many men's boyhood experience.

For the first few years of my life, I grew up in a military family, traveling abroad, although I was too young to recall much of it. But I do recall a lot of raucous and rowdy behavior on the part of my parents. I grew up with both parents working, so there was very little supervision. I went through two divorces with my parents; I was sexually molested before the age of 10; I was exposed to pornography at an early age; I was abusing marijuana when I was a pre-teen; I was severely abusing alcohol as an early teen; I was in disciplinary trouble at school; I was shop-lifting, stealing cars, breaking into houses; and I was sexually promiscuous, all before I was 18. I eventually went on to abuse cocaine, get arrested for drunk driving (a military arrest), and get married and divorced, all by the time I was 23 years old. And it didn't look much better from 23 to 32, when some things changed in my life (more on my life later in the book).

I know that some of you can relate to the brief description of my adolescence. Some of you knew "boys like me," but were shocked to know some kids grew up this way. Some of you, tragically, only dreamed of having it as good as I did. My experience, and those worse than mine, are a modern-day (post-industrial age era) phenomenon. Unfortunately, for baby-boomer fathers and younger, like myself, we may not realize that this was not always normal in our society, because it has been our norm. In many cases, our experiences were not that much different than other boys, causing us to just think this was a normal adolescent experience.

However, another type of home that is equally, if not more, damaging to our boys and our society is the one that produces an apathetic man, maybe not even really a man at all by my definition. This type of home merely provides a coddling, caretaking, protective, unaccountable, developmental (emotional and maturity) retardation of boys in America. The young man from this type of home was protected from all things uncomfortable and disagreeable. He didn't have to do much of anything, as nearly all things were done for him: from folding his clothes and putting them away for him, to making his lunches for school when he was capable, to allowing him to come and go as he pleased. This boy had no boundaries or expectations imposed on him or enforced, and he did not experience any real consequences for his behavior, nor any real accountability. In this home, the boy may frequently have seen others blamed for his problems by his parents, and he rarely had to accept any responsibility. Often this was the result of an unhealthy and a overpowering maternal presence, along with an underrepresented paternal presence in the boy's life.

Today, I am happily married to the same woman I divorced at 23, and we are about to celebrate our 27th anniversary. I have three amazing children: Devan, age 19, Brendan, age 17, and ClaraAnn, age 13. I have had multiple careers, but ultimately co-founded a small consulting and training company that had reasonable success for 12 years. I am now a licensed minister and a staff pastor at a local Christian church. I have a fantastic marriage that gets better with time; my kids are amazing and haven't done any of the things that I did. In fact, as adolescents, they are quite literally the antithesis of me, and have only brought my wife and I joy. And much to my own surprise at times, I find myself writing a book on raising sons. As I have said to many people, my boys included, I have learned how to do a few things right, and I know from experience how to do a whole lot of things wrong. Hopefully, the blending of those two will be helpful to you as you take on the noble, critical, and urgent task of raising real boys to be real men.

MY PURPOSE

There are more good books on raising boys and parenting than I can count. I discover more every day, and this is not a parenting book *per se*. So why am I writing a book on the subject? I believe that where I may have a similar position to some authors, or where I am in lock step with others, or in some cases in complete contradiction with some books and their authors, my journey has led me to focus my book on a process, intentionality, being purposeful. I have discovered that knowledge, information gathering in and of itself, rarely produces change. What I hope to achieve with my book is moving past just gathering information, or knowing what to do with a boy. My goal is to move fathers to intentional, purposeful action, or actions, that create change and lead to a predetermined outcome – a young man, prepared and ready to go into the world and be a positive force – through a rite of passage. Most likely, this will be in stark contrast to how he was raised.

You may already know a bit about raising a son properly; you may have had or seen some good models, listened to radio or talk shows, read some books, heard it in church, or sat through parenting classes. There is no shortage of good information, or bad information, for that matter. But there is a gap in execution. I hope to help you: a) sort through the information and experience you have received, decide properly what is helpful, and what needs to go to the trash bin; and b) put it all into a process (a rite of passage) that helps you to act intentionally. I hope to help close that gap.

MEN, WE HAVE A CRISIS!

I am a firm believer in the people. If given the truth, they can be depended upon to meet any national crisis. The great point is to bring them the real facts.

– Abraham Lincoln

THE ENEMY IS AT THE DOOR

Men, we have a crisis, whether you realize it or not. Some of the indicators that identify we are in crisis in the Unites States are, in part, reflected in the points below:

- The lack of leadership and moral courage in every institution;
- The degradation of our society through the deterioration of traditional values, the guardians for our society;
- The destruction of the structure and order, and the ongoing attempt to redefine the traditional family;
- An economy that has hovered on collapse for years, and a country that appears so confused from the outside that we must look schizophrenic;
- Runaway crime, behavior that borders on anarchy at times, and a depressing increase in every statistic that indicates a growing amoral population (having no moral standards, restraints, or principles; unaware of or indifferent to

questions of right or wrong).

The result is the extraordinarily low state of our social, political, economic, cultural, familial, and spiritual condition in the United States today. I believe that these points of concern are rooted in a slowly developing phenomenon with disastrous consequences. It is the transformation and decline of the definition and role of men in our society.

The role of men used to be characterized as noble, character-driven, courageous, strong, and dependable. Where men were once relied upon to lead – beginning with leading ourselves, then our families, and outward from there – they have become increasingly self-centered, immature, and irresponsible. Rather than being the guardians for our society, men have increasingly become the problem in our society. Statistics can be boring, but they can also be very telling. I recommend Michael Gurian's book entitled *The Good Son;*[1] below are some statistics from it to illustrate my point. The book was published a little over 10 years ago. Upon doing my own research in regard to these statistics for 2012, I found they have not changed much over time. Some have gone up a little, some have gone down a little, but generally the statistics have not moved favorably over the last decade:

- We have the most violent non-war population of children in the world. More people in the U.S. per capita commit violent crimes every day than anywhere else, and 90 percent of them are male.
- More of our children per capita get arrested for crimes than in any other country. Ninety percent of arrestees are boys.
- After Russia, more of our citizens are in prison than in any other country in the world. Ninety percent of these

incarcerated individuals are males.

- Our young males make up 80 percent of drug-addicted and alcoholic youth.
- Our boys constitute the majority of children who are homeless, murdered, in foster care, neglected and institutionalized.
- Our rate of mental disorders in the male population per capita is one of the highest in the world. For instance, 90 percent of the Ritalin used on children in the world is used on ours. Approximately 3,000,000 kids are on Ritalin in the U.S. – 90 percent of them are boys.
- The child suicide rate has gone up in recent decades with increasing acceleration, mainly among adolescent boys.
- Our teen pregnancy rates are among the highest in the industrialized world, and we provide the *least* extended family support for teens that have babies. Ninety percent of males who impregnate a teen girl abandon her and her family.
- Our schoolchildren are arguably the least disciplined in the world. Ninety percent of the children who require discipline in schools are boys. As one educator put it, "After teaching in Hong Kong, Japan and Australia, then returning to the United States, I felt something like despair when I saw what had happened in the American middle school class room."
- Our boys and young men also comprise the majority of child-abuse victims and are less likely to talk about, and get help for their suffering. In a 1998 study of 7,000 children, 48 percent of boys, compared to 29 percent of girls, said they would never tell anyone about the abuse they had experienced. As psychologist Aaron Kipnis explains: "It's egodystonic – not in accord with their self-image and

traditional gender identity – for boys to complain about pain." Thus, our boys are becoming more and more at risk for abuse, neglect, violence, addiction, psychological illness, and all the pains of childhoods lived in broken homes and confusing worlds, pains that never appear in statistics.

CASES IN POINT

Story #1: A family has the 23-year-old son still living at home. He dropped out of high school in his junior year. He has not held any real job at all since that time. He is living, and has lived this entire time, in his parent's basement, with the exception of a six-month hiatus in which he found the real world a little too mean and challenging, and then he returned home. He doesn't clean up after himself. The basement is a pigsty, with dirty dishes, garbage, and clothes everywhere. He has a computer, watches TV, and plays video games all day long. He doesn't pay rent or any part of his living expenses. Finally, he doesn't even take the time to go upstairs to use the bathroom; he will simply step out the door of the basement and urinate in the drain. The stepfather is completely exasperated. The mother and stepfather are on the verge of divorce. The whole family is disintegrating, and they don't know what to do. The man-child's response, sitting and listening to all this, is a few shrugs, minor acknowledgements, passive pathetic looks, and an occasional slightly embarrassed smile.

Story #2: A family has two college-aged boys living at home. One dropped out of college, and the other kicked out because of poor academic performance. Neither is working consistently, nor paying for rent or sharing with other expenses. One has been arrested six times for drug possession. With the help of his mother, he spends what money he makes on attorneys to stay out of jail.

The other son spends what little money he has on cell phones, clothes, and social activities. Neither of them has saved anything, paid anything, or has a plan to get out. The father says he doesn't know what to do, because he never imagined his grown sons dropping out and living at home. The mother is fearful of what will happen to them if she doesn't allow them to stay. Both boys smirk, nod, laugh, and justify their activities, as their story is being shared with a national audience. The lack of remorse, shame, or embarrassment is revealing as to the condition of these young men's attitudes and state of mind.

These two scenarios are not stories made up for the sake of my book; they are not exaggerated illustrations to make a point. These are two real-life current realities that my wife and I watched on The Doctor Phil show recently. On one hand, I was dumbfounded as I watched these stories unfold before my eyes. However, on the other, I was not surprised when I saw the behavior of the parents, particularly of the father figures. The fathers had completely abdicated their leadership role and were failing both as fathers and husbands. Are these examples anomalies?

Unfortunately, they are not. I see it every day professionally, and just simply living in America today; running into these caricatures of men is unavoidable. This destructive trend of boy-men not voluntarily leaving home, or not being made to leave home, not experiencing life's realities and struggles to learn and grow and mature, is not good, and it's rising at an alarming rate. The result: weak men.

These are just a couple of examples of what has gone wrong with our sons; really, examples of what has gone wrong with us as fathers. This has resulted in what we are seeing with our sons. I have sat with many parents who want help figuring out how to recover with their adult sons, or the runaway behavior of teens. I have sat with innumerable men, 20-somethings and up, single, married, divorced, some with children already. All have one thing in common: they know their life is broken, but they don't know how to get it right after years, or decades, of dysfunction. I have seen and heard it all. It ranges from horrific abuse to absolute neglect to crippling coddling, causing delayed emotional development and maturity.

These parents, and specifically fathers, did not intend to create these poor results with their sons. Who would do that intentionally to their sons, or themselves? Maybe these scenarios hit close to home for you. If so, you are not alone, and there is hope for you, and, by extension, for the sons you are raising. Let this awareness be an awakening, a catalyst to inspire you to learn how to adjust and make course corrections. The natural state of things in nature is decay, and if we do nothing, continued decay will be the result with our sons and our culture. The purpose of this book is to raise awareness, provide you with hope, and then help you with a road map to a solution.

Returning to the illustration of the eagle, the reality provided by nature gives us some excellent examples and lessons to consider as we think about the scenarios. I personally believe there is an active agent behind nature, but for now, nature gives us the eagle as a teaching tool. The contrasts between the previous stories and the eagle are obvious, and don't need to be stated. What should be even more compelling to us is that both (the scenarios and nature's examples) are real.

IGNORANCE IS NOT BLISS

Before we go any further, we must first understand the urgency of our current situation. The illustrations above are all well and good, but why should it matter to you and to me? There is a reality for all of us fathers; we have a crisis on our hands, a storm is brewing. As people, we generally fall into one of three categories:

1. Those fully aware, who know something must be done;
2. Those somewhat aware, who simply hope the problem will go away; and
3. Those completely unaware, who are blindsided.

Whatever category you fit into, the reality of something coming isn't diminished simply because you don't see it, or hope it just goes away. History can be a great teacher, although all too often it repeats itself. There are some significant traumatic events in our history from which to learn. Regardless of the level of awareness of men at the time, the following events still occurred, resulting in significant negative consequences. In the late 1930s and early part of the 1940s prior to World War II, there was a storm brewing in Europe, and it caught us. In the late 1960s and early 1970s, there was a storm brewing in Southeast Asia, and it caught us. In the late 1990s and early 2000s, there was an economic storm brewing on Wall Street that caught us. In 2000 and 2001, prior to September 11th, 2001, there was another storm brewing in the Middle East, and it caught us. You may personally not have been able to do anything about WWII, Vietnam, the stock market collapse, or September 11th, but there is another storm brewing you can do something about. It's a crisis in manhood. This might sound alarmist, but it's with good cause.

In my years as a business consultant, we often used root cause analysis, which is essentially a process to analyze a problem by gathering information from many different and divergent sources (data and feedback). Once you have good data, you ask the right questions to ensure you are dealing with the real core cause of a problem in order to solve it, once and for all. If you skip this step, you may chase and treat symptoms of the problem and never actually deal with the real cause. It will continue to rear its ugly head, wasting valuable time and causing frustration for all.

There is another term we use in business when selling – it's called opportunity cost. It simply refers to the opportunity that is lost, which cannot be recovered, if a business fails to act now. In business, it can mean loss of revenue, cost savings, competitive advantage, and more. In business, it's very real and is taken seriously. With our sons, the opportunity cost is huge, and much like business, there are opportunities that are lost that cannot be recovered.

How in the world did I go from eagles, to World War II and September 11th, to root cause analysis and opportunity cost? Am I ADD? Well, yes, probably a little bit. But that is not why. As a father, you must consider your:

- *Awareness* (WWII, September 11th, etc). There is a sense of urgency you need to be awakened to, and you must be *aware* that the true enemy to your sons comes in unexpected ways while you are being duped into complacency, distracted by the unimportant, or debating about whether the threat is your problem.
- *Responsibility* (eagle). You have a *responsibility* to raise your son in such a way that he is prepared to be a very specific kind of man, one who is properly and intentionally prepared to be released into the world, and who positively affects it.
- *Preparedness* (root cause analysis). You may ask yourself, "Am I *prepared* to deal with this problem and take it on?" If you agree with me that there is a real problem, that it is an immediate threat to you, your family, your legacy, and our society, then you better make sure you're not wasting your

time chasing symptoms, but rather dealing with the real problem.

Now some may be asking, "How do I raise my son up to be a man, when I never really had a father?" Or maybe you had a father, but he was clueless and unable to help you because he hadn't been taught. Maybe your father was tragically disinterested and disengaged, and left you to your own devices, or he was an overtly negative, destructive influence in your life, or so passive you saw nothing resembling a strong male presence, only one that acquiesced and abdicated his male role. Unfortunately, we don't often parent and raise our kids from the ideal model, taking time to observe and learn what is really right, good, healthy, and balanced. Instead, we tend either to emulate what we saw and experienced, or we parent from what was lacking in our own experience. Often, we listen to the most current trend from the hot pop psychologist, and use the great "new" idea of these so-called experts. Any one of these is a potential misstep that leads to perpetuating one form of dysfunction or another, but does not break the cycle.

We are rapidly losing good raw material for the future of our families, society, and country. In manufacturing, if you don't have good raw material to start with, you are going to produce an inferior product. Men, it is our responsibility, and no one else's, to ensure there is a large inventory of good raw material leaving home and going into the world. Our young women are looking for them, and so are their parents. Our institutions desperately need them. Our entire society is longing for them. Our current crisis demands them.

Regardless of your upbringing, if you agree with me that there is a real problem, read on. This book will help you be the solution. If you partly agree with me that there may be a problem lurking out there, but you're not sure that it's *your* problem, read on; this book will convince you and move you to action. If you disagree with me on this matter, then consider fighting the inclination to close the book and reject my premise. You may just find yourself at the end of the book asking, "What do I do next?" The clock is ticking. The storm is brewing. The question hangs ominously in the air. Will we rise up and be the men and fathers we long to be in our hearts, the ones we dare to dream about being in our quiet, honest moments? Or will we continue on the path of least resistance, denying that a crisis is coming, one that seeks out what is most dear to us, our families, our marriages, our hearts, and our homes?

WHY DO I CARE?

Failure is not fatal, but failure to change might be.

– John Wooden

A HAUNTING FEELING

Several years ago, I woke up one morning and something was nagging me, gnawing at the back of my mind. I wasn't quite able to put my finger on it, but it had something to do with my boys. I was unsettled about something. My older son, Devan, was turning thirteen, and his younger brother, Brendan, was eleven. I have a beautiful daughter as well, ClaraAnn, and she was eight at the time.

What was gnawing at me was a mild desperation, a subtle anxiety that was slowly growing. Have you ever sensed that something was coming your way, but you couldn't put your finger on it; you just "felt" it? That's what I was experiencing.

As I had a growing sense of something out in front of me, I began to ask myself some questions, and as a man of faith, I prayed. Here is what I learned. Over the course of the preceding months, I had been exposed to several different messages: a popular movie, a radio talk show, a book, a public speaker, all relating to the same general topic. The movie was *Failure to Launch*, and it glorified a grown man with a good job, a nice car, living with parents, womanizing, and living a reckless, careless, irresponsible life. The movie was funny, but the message was pathetic. The radio talk show host, sharing statistics about the increasing number of grown men that were living at home with their parents, was alarming and disconcerting. The book was about the state of our teen culture in America, which is, frankly, scary. The public speaker was talking about the absence of good male role models for young men to emulate, and how popular culture was gladly filling that void.

What this did was raise my awareness and open up my radar, in a manner of speaking; then, of course, my personal observations – what I was seeing all around me – only supported all this data that was filling my head. Today, the situation has grown so prevalent that there is a name assigned to this phenomenon: Adultolescent. This is a forgotten, but not new, term. It has been given new life and relevance in 2012. Have you seen the movie *Big* with Tom Hanks? In the movie, he is a young boy who wishes he was big, and he wakes up the next morning in the body of a man. Well, that isn't far from reality in many cases today, and that is an adultolescent. An adultolescent is simply an adolescent, someone undeveloped and immature, in an adult body. The questions began to get more succinct in my mind:

- What is happening to America?
- What is happening to families?
- What is happening to men?
- Where are the men?
- Where are the dads?

These questions were reinforced during the hours I spent counseling men, women, couples, and families – I had become acutely aware that there was a real vacuum in male leadership. It was getting more and more difficult to find truly responsible, accountable, emotionally healthy, strong men in the more traditional sense. In many cases, it wasn't that as men they didn't want to be a nobler, better version of themselves. The problem was they had no clue, because they had never been taught how. This was what was keeping me awake, haunting me, and causing me angst! My boys were on the verge of becoming men, and I wondered what kind of men they would become. After being saturated with all the messages I mentioned earlier, and realizing they were recounting the majority of my life in vivid detail (and I suspect many of yours as well), it became a compelling conviction in my heart. I had to do something different.

THE QUINTESSENTIAL ADULTOLESCENT

Like some of you, I arrived on the scene of "manhood" nothing more than an immature, ill-prepared adolescent in a grown-up man's body. I was an adultolescent; I was 18, out of high school, I was completely untrained, and I was unleashed on the world; it was time to face life.

Most of us probably didn't think of ourselves as an emerging man at that stage of our lives. We kind of thought we had arrived. Our dads may not have seen us that way, either, much less have known how to prepare us for the role. I would submit it is only because neither we, nor our fathers, had much perspective. By nature, we are all a little myopic. It's not natural to get out of our roles and holes and subject ourselves to scrutiny, apply critical thinking skills, and ask ourselves probing questions about our weaknesses. So we just simply become a product of our environment, a perpetuation or variation of what we see, what we are exposed to, and what we are immersed in.

So what became of me at 18? Most of my friends went off to college. I ended up working in a warehouse from 4:00 am to 2:00

pm going nowhere fast, not making enough money to live on my own, so I was living with my parents. I was partying with the few friends that were still around, or my new like-minded friends, blowing what little money I was making at bars, on frivolous stuff, and chasing women. Finally, out of desperation, and seeing no way out of my rut, I joined the Navy. The military was good for me in a lot of ways and taught me many things, but it did not teach me to be a man as I understand it now. It turned out to be a route that fueled my immaturity and adolescent behavior; I just had more money and a roof over my head. It created and imposed a few boundaries on me, but as much as anything, it funded and fueled my unbridled, undisciplined life of waste.

I thought being a man then was how much I could drink, how many women I could hook up with, whether I was better at demeaning my buddies than they were at demeaning me, whether I could stay out of trouble and avoid getting caught, and how much fun (as I defined it then) could I fit into a day. What was lacking was any self-discipline, any sense of vision or goals for my life, any sense of responsibility for anyone or anything. I really didn't care about, or even think about, character. I was abundantly self-serving, selfish, and self-indulgent! I didn't care about tomorrow, next month, or next year, beyond what I thought I could get out of it. I let the culture and those around me define what fun was, what maturity was, what a man was.

AN ADULTOLESCENT'S END RESULT

By the time 1996 rolled around, I was 32 years old, my wife and I were in our second round of marriage and heading full speed ahead to divorce number two. I married my wife, Donna, the first time in 1985, when I was 20 and she was 21. We had known each other only a few months. I was emotionally and psychologically immature, to say the least. Our journey from then to now included two divorces from each other, and two subsequent remarriages to each other. Yes, you heard that correctly: my wife and I have been married to each other three times, and divorced from each other twice. We have been together and married to each other for the better part of 26 years as of this writing. My wife lived and dealt with being married, divorced, and remarried: a full-on textbook description of an adultolescent, the product of our modern culture in America.

Back to age 32, we already had two sons, Devan, who was age three, and Brendan, who was one. I was in a financial mess, with a job that wasn't giving me much hope for the immediate situation or my future prospects. I tried different jobs, but couldn't get anything really good going because I didn't have enough education, although along the way I did find some good opportunities at jobs and pay. Even though I made more money, rather than being responsible and eliminating debt, I raised my lifestyle and kept on spending. I was in the same place as before, but just at a higher level. I transferred one credit card balance to another, fooling myself into thinking I was actually doing something productive. I was paying minimum payments and hoping that it would leave a few dollars on the balance that I could reuse.

I was trying to find an escape at the tavern after work, and I was driving my wife away. I clearly had no concept of leadership, or my role and responsibilities as a man, a husband, or father. I was a slightly more sophisticated adolescent, but eventually felt that same sense of hopelessness and despair. I knew something was wrong, but I seemed unable to identify it or change it. I was unhappy with my marriage (because I was unhappy with myself). My wife was unhappy in our marriage. I was drinking and hanging out in bars and taverns with the guys because I was in no hurry to get home. I was heading out on weekends to play golf and drink with my buddies. Life was spinning downward, and I was just along for the ride.

The end result was probably similar to what some of you reading this book have experienced. I woke up one day spent, broke, in debt, married, with a marginal job that I didn't enjoy, kids, and cars I could not afford, and stuck in a deep rut! I was extremely unhappy. I had no plan and no hope. I ended up in multiple divorces and facing bankruptcy, and a slow, sinking feeling of despair began to set in, somewhere deep in my gut.

THE TURN-AROUND

It was in March of 1996, stuck in the rut I called my life, when there were some dramatic and life-altering events that transformed me forever. I encountered God, I gave my life over to Jesus Christ and entered into a relationship with him – I refer to that as my birthday. I immediately started reading the Bible, which prior to this I had believed to be pure nonsense. That conversion experience and what I was discovering in the Bible, was dramatically life altering. It is difficult to explain, but have you ever read or seen something that stopped you in your tracks, where the experience left you awestruck? That is what this was like for me. For the first time I began to see and understand why my life was the way it was. It's not an easy thing to come to grips with the fact that when your life stinks and you are miserable, it was all avoidable and that you did not have to have the experiences you had. It's equally difficult to come to the point where you realize that others could have helped you avoid it altogether, chiefly your father and other men in your life, but that they did not.

However, this is not about blame, this is about personal accountability. As a grown man, I could not blame my father or anyone else, and the first step in growing up and changing anything is taking responsibility. I soon realized that my dad did the best that he could. Tragically, though, there are dads who do not give their best, even if it is errant, and that is also disastrous, because it communicates to their sons that they just don't care. A core part of the whole adultolescent phenomenon is the shifting of blame and deflecting responsibility. I had to take responsibility, if anything was going to change.

I discovered an entirely new way to live life. I was finally able to identify what was wrong; it was literally like starting life all over again, in many respects. The Bible says several things that were immediately relevant to me:

- *"I have given you the choice between life and death, between blessings and curses"* (Deuteronomy 30:19). I had a choice, and I had certainly chosen over the years, I couldn't blame anyone else at 32.
- *"There is a path before each person that seems right, but it ends in death"* (Proverbs 14:12). Sure enough, true for me again.
- *"Don't be misled – you cannot mock the justice of God. You will always harvest what you plant"* (Galatians 6:7). Again, dead on accurate for me and my life.
- *"His divine power has given to us all things that pertain to life and godliness"* (2 Peter 1:3). Over the course of my life, both outside of relationship with God, and the last 15 years of following him, I have found these things to be true.

Ultimately, I discovered how to correct what was wrong in my life. I have seen so many things in my life that could have been different, or are different now, because I have chosen to follow God's directions for my life rather than what I wanted to do. On this side of Christianity, it's a no brainer. However, on the other side, it truly does seem like foolishness (the Bible says that, as well, as I was surprised to discover).

Our culture has beaten up on Christian beliefs and values so much that most people, knowing little or nothing about the reality of it, reject it outright. I did! But from that moment on, at age 32, my life, my values, and my decision-making were all sharply influenced by a whole new view and philosophy, so different from the one I grew up with.

WHY DO I CARE?

So why do I care? What makes me so passionate about this? It is simple – compare and contrast. I have lived many years outside of Christianity, and now many years inside, applying its principles. There is only one way that is truly right, that produces an enduring legacy and creates a quality life worth living. I knew it, because I was experiencing it.

There I was, five years ago at age 42, and the impending sense that I was feeling was this: What had I done, or what am I doing, to ensure that my boys would have a different story than I did? Did I want my boys to have my experience? NO! Did I want them to squander 20 years of their lives and hope they'd figure it out someday? NO! But what was I doing other than "hoping" that it would be different? It has been said that hope is not a strategy, and it's very true. It may get you started, but it won't get you through. What was my strategy, my plan? I didn't have one, and that was what was keeping me awake at nights. My track record was not very good: two divorces, financial failure, alcohol and drug abuse, promiscuity, career failures – the list is not pretty.

How was I going to help my boys? One thing was absolutely clear to me: it was not the school's, government's, or church's responsibility to help my sons make the transition from being boys to being men. It was mine! I was a product of all those forces along with the popular culture. I could not stand the idea of my boys creating and causing the same damage, hurt, and heartache in their lives and, consequently, in the lives of their wives, kids, and all the other people they would touch, those for whom they would eventually have responsibility.

They would be my daughters-in-law someday. They would be my grandkids. They would be the kids that my heart would ache for, if I had to watch them make many self-destructive decisions that influence so many people, including their mother and me.

I had to ask myself, "What vision do I have for my boys and their future? What was I going to do to give them a fighting chance to be real men (something I will define later)"? This was my responsibility, and the more I thought about it, the more it appeared to be my most significant responsibility. After all, they are the product of their family, and most significantly, their father. Their attitudes and beliefs, their self-image and self-worth, their expectations, their sense of responsibility, their dreams, hopes, and vision would all be heavily influenced by me. I could not afford to be MIA on this assignment.

I knew right then and there I had to step up: I had to fight for my boys and their future, their families yet to be, and their legacy yet to be defined. They would not be like me and arrive on the scene without a clue, without direction. Instead, they would arrive with a plan, confidence, strength, and accountability. There is no other option. I cannot be responsible for the choices and decisions they make, but I certainly am responsible for them knowing what and how to choose and decide. That is my chief responsibility as a father. So here is a question for you, Dad: What's your vision? As a dad with boys, what's your purpose? This is a practical book, based on principles extrapolated from the Bible, that will help you raise your sons to become men. I have personally seen what can happen in just one generation. It is powerful.

I watched my dad observe his three grown children. We represent multiple broken marriages, with grandkids from these different relationships, and some grandkids not present because of strained relationships, a family that is broken, with siblings who don't want to be near each other or their parents. I watched my dad see his kids go from one mess to another, as his grown kids came in and out of his house as adults (myself included), as their relationships, finances, families, and jobs came unraveled time and again. I watched him lament that some of his kids wouldn't talk to him for reasons he didn't fully understand.

How did all this come about? How did my dad's kids' lives turn out the way they did? It was a reflection, a mirror image of my father's own life. My father reproduced unto his own kind: divorce, bankruptcy, broken families, alcohol, all of it. Not on purpose, of course. No father, mine included, who has had a difficult and painful life wants his kids to experience those things. And yet, we see it time and time again all over America, the story repeated. I knew there was a better way, but it wasn't going to happen by accident. It was only going to happen intentionally, with a plan and execution! And it had to begin with a different vision, a picture in my mind of what I wanted. This is hope's place in the equation.

Earlier I made the statement, hope is not a strategy, and it is true. However, there's no strategy without the hope that you can break the cycle that trapped the men in your family. You need hope for the motivation to begin. So let hope play its role and get you started. Let it be the catalyst that leads you to developing a real plan, and the gas in your tank to work your plan.

DO YOU HAVE A VISION?

I had to develop my own vision of what I wanted, a compelling vision that was exciting and full of life and authentic manhood on the part of my boys. I knew what I didn't want, but I learned the hard way that knowing what you don't want does not get you to where you want to go. Instead, you must know what you do want. Can you see this? I had a vision of family events at our house with our kids and their spouses. They were happily married, madly in love with their respective husband and wives. They had beautiful families, lots of kids playing with each other. My kids love each other, and they are best friends. I envision families that are financially disciplined, making good decisions and living within their means, enjoying a life free of financial stress. My wife and I are sitting on our deck; it's a sunny, warm August afternoon, the pool is open, and our grandkids are splashing and playing with their cousins. Our three grown children and their spouses are sitting together in lounge chairs laughing with each other and having a great time. My wife and I are holding hands, watching this scene in front of us, and we know this...we did well, and we did it on purpose. That is my vision, and that motivates me.

What is your vision for your family and their future? If they are young, they don't have a vision, and they certainly aren't thinking about it. And maybe, depending on their age, they don't need to. But *you* do! Someone has to have a vision, because without a vision, people, families, and nations fail (Proverbs 29:18 KJV). So get a vision!

Take a moment right now. Close your eyes. Put yourself out in the future when your boys are adults. What exactly do you want your family's future to look like? What do you want your kids' future and families to look like? Don't think too broadly; think of a specific moment in time, like I did. Mine was a summer family barbeque at our house where our kids grew up, and they bring their kids back to hang out with Grandma and Grandpa. Your past and your family's past do not have to be your future, or your kids' future. This will only happen, however, if we are intentional in helping our little men in training to successfully transition from boys to men.

It's your responsibility, dad, to get them started straight. Think of yourself as an archer (Robin Hood, maybe), and your boys as arrows. They are a sharp, penetrating point with a lot of force propelling them forward. If you don't aim it, there is no telling where that arrow will go and what damage it may do along the way. But if you aim it…wow! Now it becomes a powerful, penetrating force headed for the bull's eye and hitting the mark. The choice is yours: are you going to aim the arrow, or are you just going to let it fly off in some random direction? Those who aim at nothing will hit nothing every time, with amazing accuracy.

We know there are no guarantees. There are a lot of good men who have worked hard with their sons, but their sons went sideways for a season in life. We all have free will, and our sons will make their choices. But I will promise three things:

1. They will have a significantly better chance at a successful life if you do this.

2. If they do go sideways on you at some point, they will find their way back.

3. When all is said and done, regardless of the outcome, you will lay your head down at night, and know, it wasn't because you weren't faithful to your boys, or because you didn't give them the template and pathway to manhood. Without regret, you laid the foundation. Feel good about that and remember that they ultimately make the choices.

So that is why I care. I care about my boys. I care about my future grandchildren. I care about your boys. I care about the men they will become. I care about the field of men that my daughter, and maybe your daughter, will choose from. I care about where we will end up as a society if we don't do our part. I care about the future leaders in government, business, and church. I would like to believe there are other like-minded men to my left and right, even if I don't know you, who also care and believe that they too can make a difference. So as we close this chapter I ask you, what is your vision? What is your plan? What are you going to do to give your son a fighting chance?

HOW DID WE GET HERE?
THE LOSS OF THE RITE OF PASSAGE

✱ *A people that values its privileges above its principles soon loses both.*

– Dwight D. Eisenhower

WHEN I WAS A CHILD

If you're reading this page, that means that you can relate to my experience at least a little bit. It also means that you sincerely care about the future of your sons and your family's legacy. You are beginning to develop a burden for your son's future. You are beginning to identify what you want for him, or at least you know what you don't want, and that's a beginning! You are beginning to think purposefully and intentionally. You are fulfilling a significant portion of your purpose as a father.

There is a book in the Bible called Proverbs. It is also referred to as the Book of Wisdom. This is because it is full of wisdom about how to live our lives. It was written by King Solomon and addressed to his son – a book of wisdom from a father, based on his life, to his son, to help him have a successful life. There isn't a more precise, profound, simple, yet powerful piece of work available to fathers. As a father raising a son, Book of Proverbs is gold, a template for raising your son. King Solomon created all these short and simple bite-size nuggets of wisdom so that any man can easily chew on them. For those of you who are not familiar with Solomon, he is thought to have been the wisest man on earth. Kings and rulers throughout the known world sought his wisdom and counsel. Great homage was paid to him for his wisdom, and great prices were paid for his knowledge and experience. He wrote these proverbs around 950 B.C., and the fact that they are still extraordinarily relevant today is a further testament to his wisdom.

The primary keys for my rite of passage come primarily from the core principles of Proverbs. If they were good enough for Solomon and his sons, and God saw fit to record them, they are good enough for my sons and me. I'm confident that in reading them, you too will find that the wisdom, instruction, encouragement, and council of Solomon are spot on. If I had lived my life according to Solomon's instructions to his son, it would have been completely different, and for the better. Solomon was writing to set his son up for success, to have a quality life, a good name, and rich legacy.

One evening, my wife and I were sitting at our dinner table. We had three young couples dining with us. They were all engaged to be married, and this was their graduation for completing a pre-marriage class we teach. As we were sitting at the table finishing dinner, my older son had to leave for an event. One of the young women at our dinner had parked her car behind my son's car, and it needed to be moved so he could leave. He came into the dining room and asked whose car it was. The young woman said it was hers, and she would move it. My 16-year-old son told her that she didn't need to get up – he would move it for her. Anyway, as she was getting up from the table, I looked across at her fiancé and gave him the "eye." The "eye" clearly said, "Dude, what are you doing? Why is your fiancée getting up from the table in the cold, dark night to move her car? Get up and move her car!" He looked back at me, and his look said, "What? She can do it; she's capable."

In the meantime, my son insisted and persuaded the young woman to sit down and enjoy her dinner. My son moved the car for this young woman. And while I was very proud of my son, I was equally struck by the behavior of this 32-year-old across the table from me, her fiancé who just let another young man steal his opportunity to be her hero. He didn't care enough about his fiancée to allow her to enjoy her dinner and move her car for her. He missed a great opportunity to be the man she deserved, the man he was capable of being. It occurred to me at that moment that maybe his father had failed him. Was what I was seeing just the by-product of the previous generation perpetuated? And don't you know that the farther away the branch grows from the tree, the weaker it becomes? I was witnessing that very thing. Culturally, we have gotten far away from the authentic definition of a man and we are getting weaker by the generation.

What does this story have to do with the subject of this book, the rite of passage? Everything! For me, a rite of passage has come to mean the transition a male makes as he moves from being a boy to discovering what it means to be a man. A rite of passage is principally about developing character. I realized from this dinner experience that it wasn't entirely based on age. There are many little, but often defining, moments that are revealing about your son's character and development. The Bible puts it very pointedly: *"When I was a child I spoke like a child, I thought like a child. But when I became a man I put childish things away."* (1 Corinthians 13:11 NKJ)

It was becoming obvious to me that what I was seeing, and what we are experiencing today, is this scripture unfulfilled. We have stopped becoming men and we have retained childish thinking. **!!**

A LITTLE HISTORY

While I declare in this chapter's subtitle that in America there is no longer the rite of passage, it is important to point out that there was never a specific American rite that fathers took their boys through. Rather, the rite was something "caught" by a boy through the process of osmosis. In America, in the not-so-distant past (from our founding until the early 1800s), this was facilitated in the way we lived, a way of life that has long since passed away and ushered in an entirely new society. I read a fantastic book by Tom Brokaw called *The Greatest Generation*[1]. This helped me to clarify, at least in part, how this loss occurred.

There is a remarkable contrast between the generation that went to war in the mid 1940s and the subsequent ones. It is such a stark difference that one has to wonder what things would look like now if we understood what they understood then. I think that generation was most clearly defined by its values. There was a very sharp line drawn between how that generation grew up and every generation since World War II. Obviously, some of what has changed is good; I'm not throwing the baby out with the bath water. But much of what has changed has not been good.

Just a couple hundred years ago, it was not uncommon to see very young families in America, as young men took on responsibilities that today would seem absurd to us, if not illegal or seemingly dangerous. Prior to the industrial revolution, we were a largely agrarian society, with a strong family structure and order. That revolution brought about dramatic shifts in values and attitudes about family, roles, and society. Sociologists have arguably identified a turning point around the industrial revolution for family structure and order. During that era there was extensive exploitation of women and children in labor. Work became completely different than that in any time prior to the revolution.

The purpose and nature of work changed. Work had previously been something a family did together, learned together, and was vested in together. The father was a constant and very familiar presence and influence. A son grew up next to his father, shoulder-to-shoulder learning about life and all it entailed.

With the industrial revolution, men left their homes for the first time to go to work. They worked long hours, and the nature of their worked changed from what it had traditionally been. Families that could afford to have just the father working did so, creating the term "bread winner," which we use today. We also saw the development of the "middle class." At this point in our history, we see a diminishing of the traditional role of the father in the life of his sons. And in the cases where mothers did not work, they began to become the stronger influence in the boys' lives.

World War I followed this in the early 1900s. This escalated the social changes with families and women in the workplace. This was also the first time in an industrial age when fathers went away for long periods of time to fight in the war. Many did not come back, and many came back maimed and wounded, creating a lot of single mothers. This was followed only a decade later by the Great Depression. This again was an extraordinarily challenging time for families and society, and produced long-lasting changes in how we view society, family roles, and responsibilities. The by-product of the Depression was a collective move away from personal responsibility for our welfare, and we began putting government social safety nets in place. Although these have done some good, at the same time they have caused extraordinary harm to American society.

Finally, right on the heels of the Great Depression, we had World War II. The consequence to families as a result of this war, with absent fathers in massive numbers during the war, and then the resultant deaths from battle, or trauma from the experience, with men coming home emotionally scarred, was enormous. When men came home from World War II, they were often different than how they went. The exposure to the atrocities and hardships of war took their toll; many of these men were never the same, emotionally or physically, with their families. There was a "distance" that emerged in these men's relationships due to a lack of emotional and physical connection.

There was a great pace and scope of change, relatively speaking, which had dramatic social consequences. I believe these events created two important consequences we see today:

1. An attitude that is expressed in the idea that our kids must have it better than us.
2. A significant shift in the role and influence of fathers and mothers.

I believe that these experiences largely contributed to a prevailing attitude or belief that we need to protect our children. I don't mean protect them from predators, danger, etc. – that is every parent's responsibility. What I mean is that we began to protect them from hardship and difficulty, challenge and adversity, to elevate their comfort and shield them. We wanted to ensure our kids did not go without and were not exploited. The exploitation of children in labor, watching children suffer during the Depression, watching their family's sacrifice and privation during the war, I believe these experiences were firmly in the psyche of parents; they experienced it and watched it.

Simultaneously, as mothers played an extremely significant role in the lives of boys, the overexposure to the mother and the diminished exposure to the father created a shift in our society that has forever affected us. Fathers came home tired and exhausted, or during wartime, did not come home at all. Mothers became more and more significant and dominant in young, developing boys' lives. Fathers didn't have the same time for their boys, and we began to lose an important anchor in our societal structure.

There may not have necessarily been an intentional "passage" for boys to men prior to all this change (although in some instances there were). Nevertheless, how the family was ordered and how a boy lived alongside his father provided a structure for a boy to understand what it meant to be a man, what the responsibilities were. It also enabled the early assumption of those responsibilities. With the transition in our society, the rite of passage, the process of training to be a man, whether intentional or by osmosis, went away over the decades. These boys were slowly losing the natural transition from boyhood to manhood that taught them the significant roles, attitudes, behaviors, and responsibilities that were part of being a man. They were also losing the traditional identity of what a man was.

CURRENT REALITY

Early in the spring of 2011, there was a controversial printed advertisement by a major trendy clothing line (J. Crew) that showed a young, fair-haired boy with his mom. He looked very "soft" and "cute," and he was laughing while his mother was painting his toenails neon pink. All this was portrayed as perfectly natural. The woman is actually the little boy's mother. She is a senior executive of J. Crew. The caption for the ad read "Lucky for me, I ended up with a boy whose favorite color is pink."

There was quite a lot of commentary on this commercial, and anyone who publicly positioned themselves critically against the feminization of boys was vilified by popular culture icons. As I write, the woman has reportedly filed for divorce from her husband, and she is romantically involved with another woman. Why do I use this as an example? Because I think it illustrates a strategy and an agenda. A few decades ago that boy would have been depicted with his dad working or playing. He would have been with his buddies playing, getting dirty, getting hurt, and being a boy. The problem is not just that men have lost their way and that boys are losing a sense of themselves, women have also lost their way, and our sons are innocently caught up in the middle of it. Male and female roles have always been, and continue to be, defined in our children's minds at an early and impressionable age. If we were to go back in time and see how boys grew up only a few decades ago, in the '30s, '40s and '50s, and then to see how they grow up now, we would notice such a dramatic shift that it would be plainly obvious why we have seen such a decline in American society today. The traditional, natural and healthy male and female roles have been, and continue to be, intentionally redefined.

There are so many other examples of the serious degradation of the role of men in our culture: television's depiction of men as stupid, ignorant, grunting idiots, or sex-crazed morons, or guys who can't seem to do anything other than be crude and childish. The term "Mooks" was created a decade ago to describe this concept of the American male. Originating from a term coined by Douglas Rushkoff in an episode of PBS's "Frontline" entitled "The Merchants of Cool,"[3] Mooks are archetypal young males who act like moronic boneheads. They are self-centered simpletons who live a drunken frat-boy lifestyle. It has been argued by some critics, Rushkoff included, that Mooks are simply a creation of the media that young men bought into, and it became a self-fulfilling prophecy. This idea has been perpetuated by shows such as Family Guy, Two and A Half Men, and the like.

When you link all that we have talked about together so far - grown men living at home, not taking on responsibility, becoming increasingly self-indulgent, the changes that have occurred in our society and family order in the last century, the growing apathy of fathers, the statistics about our current situation with our kids, the story above about the J. Crew ad and its larger implications, the advent of Mooks - you have some very powerful and compelling evidence. I believe there is both an aggressive and strategic agenda to redefine and reshape masculinity, and a passivity and apathy on the part of fathers that is simultaneously weakening our young men. The results are already devastating to our society, but worse, they have the ability to be catastrophic for our society. We need to raise and train our boys to be men again.

In our continuing progression toward protecting our kids and providing a more comfortable life for them, we have, in a sense, castrated our boys. We have taken away both their opportunity and the challenge of stepping into manhood, of learning from the harshness of life, the lessons of hard work and struggle, the reality of failure and recovery, the consequences of choices, the importance of patience and delayed gratification, and of assuming the traditional role as a man. Maybe the most recent example of this "castration," the manifestation of this coddling attitude, was in 2010, when our own government continued to be complicit. Our Federal government passed legislation that redefined a child eligible for his parent's health care coverage as 26 years of age. Twenty-six years old and you are still legally considered your parent's child.

This shift has many consequences. There are two, in particular, that have been dramatic as we begin the 21st Century. The first is the one just discussed, the feminization of the male role. The other is that the definition of manhood has been confined just to physical development, that is, growing hair, noticing girls, sexual desires, etc. For many young boys, manhood means nothing more than "sowing their oats," and the more conquests they make the more of a "man" they are. The idea of being a man has somehow been reduced to a physiological and sexual context. So much so that, in the extreme, this becomes the definition of a man, and for a woman, all he's really necessary for is reproduction. Of course, nothing could be further from the truth.

Today, we see women who are desperately looking for a "grown up man," and yet time and time again, all they find are boys in men's bodies. They lack vision, goals, responsibility, dignity, character, chivalry, ethics, and courage. They have a completely distorted perspective of love, and many times, a perverted view of women. Often they lack any kind of example of what a real man is or does. Because of this lack of authentic men, young women and girls have lowered their standards and expectations.

Boys don't see their fathers opening their mother's door, or pulling out her chair. They don't see a father adoring their mother. They don't see their father protecting their mother and family, creating an environment that is safe for Mom and the kids. All too often, they see a dad that is too busy working or playing to spend quality time with his wife or family. They see a father with nude centerfold pictures hanging up in the garage. They may observe their father hanging out with his buddies, drinking and cursing, and telling sexually degrading or racial jokes. They don't see the value of commitment and faithfulness, kindness and courage toward family, and toward the most vulnerable, women. Maybe they observe a father with no sense of self-control who spoils himself, and maybe his kids, but fails to demonstrate personal financial responsibility. They may watch their parents at neighbors' parties getting drunk and getting a little wild. Way too often, they find out their father is having an affair, and as a result, their family is shaken to the core.

MY REALITY

As I share my own life experiences, I want to be very clear that I am not beating up on my dad. I love my dad, and he did the best he knew how. In fact, my dad and I have had very candid conversations, and he gets very emotional when he talks about how I am raising my boys. My dad also gave his life to Jesus Christ and became a Christian a few years after me. He has become a phenomenal grandfather, and I am honored that my kids know him as Grandpa, and as my dad. However, the reality is that both our lives, mine and my dad's, were shaped and influenced the same way, by our fathers and by our culture.

I was one of these boys shaped by the culture. I thought being a man was simply the ability to get an erection, and then trying to find a place for it. I saw my dad drink and party, so I drank and partied. I was exposed to pornography very early, and that is how I developed my attitudes about women. I saw other adult males in my family smoke pot, so I smoked pot. And there is much more we could talk about: money matters, values, ethics, character, integrity, and so on.

I was over-sexualized; I was under-educated. I had not seen the right stuff modeled, and I was not protected from the corrupting elements of popular culture. What a recipe for disaster! I had a sexual appetite that couldn't be satisfied, and my only reason for treating a girl "right" was to get something. I had no clue on how to treat a woman properly, let alone any notion of how to respect her as someone equal in value and significance. I had no sense of responsibility, no vision for my future, no care for my character, nor a good reputation. I was a self-gratifying machine. What mattered was my own gratification and self-indulgence.

But in reality, my dad didn't get any training, either; there was no rite of passage for him, no formal training on what it meant to be a man. Additionally, my dad came into his young adult years in the '60s, and raised his kids in the '70s and '80s. Those were interesting years in the cultural history of America; it was a time when a lot of traditions were recklessly discarded as old-fashioned and archaic. Now fast forward. I'm 20 and getting married. I am nothing more than an adolescent in an adult body. It is still all about my self-gratification and self-indulgence. A few years later I have my first son, and it's still all about me. Then I have my second son, and it's still all about me. What was the end of all of this for me? How about two divorces, multiple jobs, a financial nightmare, a drinking problem, and a rage problem!

There I was at 32 years old, and I didn't have a clue. My life was a mess, and I didn't know how to fix it. I knew one thing for sure: if I had it all to do over, I would do it differently. But what would I do differently? I didn't know, and that is the shame of it all. Because I didn't know, I did it over and over again, with the same end result. I hoped for something different, but remember – hope is not a strategy. I was insane by this definition: Insanity is doing the same thing over again but expecting different results.

I may not have understood it then, but working with men today and being a dad myself, it's easy to see how they get washed away with the tide of culturally acceptable behavior. It's not easy being a dad, and it is especially challenging when you decide to be a great dad who is going to be counter-culture and raise great men. You will feel like the Spartans in the movie *300*: a few strong men, fighting against the massive Persian army at the Battle of Thermopylae; they just keep coming, and they are relentless.

Fifteen years later and I'm writing this book. My marriage is restored. I have three beautiful kids, my family rocks, and my then 16-year-old young man knows how to gently tell a woman to stay at the table and enjoy her dinner – he'll move her car for her. That was definitely not me at 16! But it was my son.

Mel Gibson starred in a movie years ago called *What Women Want*. It was a funny movie, but it's not a mystery what women want. If they are candid with you, they will tell you that they are frustrated. Everywhere they encounter another character from Matthew McConaughey's movie *Failure to Launch* – a bunch of self-indulgent adultolescents that don't have a clue. Women are looking for real men, even if they don't know it yet. Our society and culture are suffering from the absence of real men. As important pillars in American society, families are perishing today because of the absence of real men. We see moral failures at the highest levels of leadership in our families, business, and government; we see undisciplined and reckless decisions with money, character, and culture all around us.

If you don't believe me, come to the mall with me some day. Watch the reaction from women when my sons open a door for them coming into or out of the mall. They gush effusively over the boys; some are shocked, most are grateful, and my sons are just opening a door! The one exception is women under 25. Generally speaking, some seem indifferent to a sincere act of kindness toward them. In some instances, they act as if some violation has just occurred, and they look quizzically as if to say, "What are you doing?" They have already been immunized against proper male behavior.

THE RITE OF PASSAGE
FINDING OUR WAY AGAIN

We all want progress, but if you're on the wrong road, progress means doing an about-turn and walking back to the right road; in that case, the man who turns back soonest is the most progressive.

– C.S. Lewis

WHAT IS A RITE OF PASSAGE?

Let's talk about the concept of a rite of passage. This is important, because I believe this is the antidote. This is what you are going to design, if you have the vision, courage, and discipline. What is a rite of passage? There are lots of ideas and concepts based on culture, attitudes, and experiences. Our definition will be this:

✤ *A deliberate, thoughtful process by which a boy is equipped to successfully engage and properly navigate the transition to manhood, to intentionally fulfill a specifically defined role as a man, in order to live and lead himself, his family, and his peers well.*

Remember from the previous chapter, 1 Corinthians, chapter 13, verse 11: *"When I was a child I spoke like a child, I thought like a child. But when I became a man I put childish things away."*

In native or indigenous cultures in different parts of the world, there are very significant rites of passage. They tend to be short in duration and intense in their nature. But they all have one thing in common: it is the time that a family and a society and culture say to a young person, "It's time to grow up."

Many are familiar with the Jewish custom of bar mitzvah for boys, and bat mitzvah for girls. This is steeped in tradition and significance. And if we look historically at the Jews, there was a time when young men, in particular, took on great responsibility for their families. There was a very intentional plan for modeling and teaching to prepare the boy to be a man and take on the impending responsibilities. It was a sharply different culture from today's. It was agrarian (based on agriculture and farming) and there was a multi-generational interdependence. Although the particulars have changed over millennia, the principles remain. A man's son and his life, his behaviors, and choices all were a reflection on the father and a part of his legacy, and they all had a profound impact on the family. The father cared about how his name was represented, and that doesn't appear to be as important in America today as it once was.

Other cultures, going back thousands of years, have their own rites of passage. They are all considerably more intense in nature and radically different from the Jewish tradition. Many rites of passage revolved around puberty. These rites also typically signaled a tribe's acknowledgement that its young women or young men had reached the age of responsibility, fertility, and community productivity, and these rites made an indelible impression on the participant. Puberty rites, which took on a variety of forms, have been well-documented and analyzed. They were intentional, designed to mold and educate the young man and prepare him for his new role in life.

Some rites involved mutilation: scarring, piercing of body parts, and tattooing, all endured in silence. Others revolved around endurance: beating, rigorous fasting, trials of pain, and seclusion. As odd as this seems to us, for them it provided a structure for young people to work within, to grow within, and to help them understand the demands of being a man. Common to all types of rites is the specific instructions from the elders about sacred law, daily life, and tribal legends. Honor, loyalty, respect, and how these might be maintained or breached were shared with the young people. They were initiated into adult privilege, but it only came as they accepted adult responsibilities.

Here is an examples. In one South American aboriginal culture, the boys sleep in the same dwelling with the women and children. Then one night, the men of the village, who sleep in a separate hut, "steal" the boy away. The women are fully aware of what is happening and the whole thing is staged. The mother will put up a mock fight for the boy. The boy is then taken into the jungle. There he is on his own in the stark, cold, and harsh wild to fend for himself. He has to fight off wild beasts, find his food, make his shelter, and so on. He is completely on his own. Or so he thinks. What he doesn't know is that the elders of the village are off in the distance, watching him and protecting him.

They will allow certain dangers to come close and some harm to come to him, but they will not allow him to be seriously hurt. At the end of the week, the boy has proven himself worthy to be a man in their culture. He has passed his "rite of passage" to manhood in his village. He returns to the village a little worse for the wear, but with a confidence and knowledge that he is a "man." As he enters the village, the elders all stand in a line with their legs spread wide apart. The young man crawls between the legs of the elders as he enters the village to demonstrate, symbolically, the passage. When he enters the village, all the women turn their backs on the young man. This is intentional and communicates that he has changed, he is not the boy he was when he left, and they don't recognize the new man that has entered the village. He left as a boy, but has come back as a man. Finally, the last woman who sees him is his mother, and she also turns her back on her son to signify how dramatically different he is now. From that point on, he sleeps with the men.

Native Americans have rites of passage ceremonies. Many African cultures have rites of passage ceremonies. Aboriginals in Australia have rites of passage ceremonies. I love movies. Not only are they entertaining, but they can also give us powerful images and stir us up. If you watched the movie *Australia,* you saw the significance of the rite of passage, or in *300,* you saw a Spartan rite of passage ceremony. If you watched *The Patriot,* you saw a strong picture of how a boy grew up in America as compared to today.

A SLOW DEATH

Most progressive cultures, for lack of a better word, have neglected to hold onto many traditions and values, and the tradition of rites of passage is no exception. They became less and less mainstream, and more and more isolated events. What happened in western culture (not just America) that so dramatically changed a long-held tradition by virtually every other culture? I believe, like so many other things, it has been swallowed up by progress, and the traditional idea of a rite of passage lost its relevance in our modern society. I think it was disregarded by what is thought to be a sophisticated society, one that often recklessly, or thoughtlessly, casts off ideas and attitudes it feels are old-fashioned or outdated. For sure, there are some things that fit that criteria and are legitimately no longer relevant, but as Tom Brokaw points out in *The Greatest Generation,* some things, many things, have transcendent value.

A son has often disregarded the sage wisdom of his father, only later to discover that he did not know it all, and his father did, in fact, know what he was talking about. Our society has had the same attitude that a young child often has, and has, to its own detriment, disregarded the wisdom of our forefathers. What about America? Up until the industrial revolution, a boy worked on the farm or land with his father. They were shoulder to shoulder. The boy lived alongside his father and learned what it meant to be a man: to work, have honor, integrity, and responsibility. There may not have been a formal rite of passage, although at times there were, but it was clear when a boy took on the responsibilities of a man, and he was fully prepared for it.

Over the last couple of centuries, the rite of passage has been marginalized and forgotten. An aggressive agenda, the one I outlined earlier, by our popular culture over the last few decades has actively worked at eroding the traditional ideas of gender and roles. Although the rite of passage was not a specific target, it was a casualty. And what allowed this to occur, what we are really talking about, is a lack of leadership on the part of men and fathers. In case you haven't noticed, men, if we don't get out in front and lead our sons, someone else will. And very likely, we are not going to enjoy much of that journey. My parents did not get in front of me and lead and guide me. Consequently, I didn't enjoy much of that journey, my parents for sure did not, and ultimately, neither did my wife after she attached herself to me.

It's been a slow death, to be sure. And the interesting thing about slow death or deterioration is that we don't notice that it is dying. We just wake up one morning and notice there has been a dramatic change. We exclaim, "Wow, what happened? You seemed just fine not that long ago." How many things in your life have you simply not paid attention to and they died over time: a plant, a car, a pet, your health, your marriage, your life, your son's life? We understand slow death.

A MODERN DAY INCARNATION

Let's talk about you and your son(s), and how to teach him what it means to be a man. Given the absence of the rites of passage in our culture today, I began to think about my life, and all the uncomfortable failures and false starts. I began to conduct a thoughtful and thorough assessment. I did a little root cause analysis, and calculated the lost opportunity cost of my life. The purpose of all this self-reflection was to come up with something that offered a real solution. I had to understand the problem before I could do anything to address it. I also spent many hours with men who have successfully raised their sons, and I read and studied about successful fathers. However, it was obvious to me: although we had certainly lost the idea, practice, and value of the traditional rite of passage, simply going back in time and resurrecting what was and bringing it into the 21st Century was not the antidote.

We live in a world that is dramatically different and more complex today, one that moves much faster. In my lifetime, I have been on the receiving end, and been the perpetrator myself, of the "ready, fire, aim" approach to life. How about you? That would not be, could not be, my approach in creating this rite of passage, or in raising my sons in the 21st Century.

However, many of the things that are good, helpful, and profitable to us in life today are not new – they are very old. The core concept has remained the same, but these things have changed and have been adapted to remain effective and useful. Financial planning, for example, is a good core principle, but from saving to borrowing to investments, it looks very different today than, say

200 years ago, when people stuffed their money in their mattresses. Automobiles are another example. We love them, we need them, but how effective would it be to reintroduce the Model T in the 21st Century? The concept is intact, but it has evolved. A modern-day incarnation of the rite of passage, in my opinion, has to undergo the same evolution.

As we define what a rite of passage is in our modern culture, we must also define what a man is, as it gives us a target for our rite of passage. How about a good, working definition of a real man? A clear picture for a father to direct his son toward. Something for both of them to aspire to that demands the very best part of both of them. So what is a good working definition of a real man? You have your own ideas shaped by your experiences, your attitudes, popular culture, movies, and religion. Maybe like me, your definition is more deeply influenced by faith, values, and the older traditions discarded years ago by our culture. Recall the definition of a real man I provided in the Foreword of this book:

> *Strong in character and tender in nature; courageous at heart and compassionate in deed; gentle in speech, but confident in action; meek in his attitude, but tenacious in his conviction; he lives life fully, but selflessly, putting himself second to all things important; he loves his wife second only to his God; he will lay his life down for his family and friends, this man leaves no one behind. He lives with a purpose larger than his life; he is a values-driven man whose name is beyond reproach, he is known for his integrity; his wife adores him; his kids honor and respect him; his friends trust and admire him. He is a man of his word.*

How would our families, our culture, our institutions, and society be affected if this were the standard man walking around today? How would you like this to be the description of *your* son?

There was a time when this was the basic calling card for a man; it was the norm and not the exception. We have wandered far from this ideal. But we can get it back, one son at a time.

Through this process of research, assessment, study, and preparation for my sons, I have created what I believe is a modern-day rite of passage. I have held to the tradition, core principles, and purpose of the rite. However, I have adapted it to the dramatically more complex world that you and I, and our sons, inhabit. I identified what I believe are nine keys, core principles, for a young man to master, or at least be proficient in, in order to be a great husband and father, and a great man, building his base in the 21st Century.

LIFE IS LIKE YOUR BIKE WHEEL

I use the analogy of a bicycle wheel to describe my rite of passage, because it seems to provide the best visual to help us understand the significance of these principles. A wheel has two vital components, the hub, which is the core, and the spokes. If the core is defective or not working properly, then not much else matters; the wheel isn't going to function properly. It's not going to roll well, if at all. The spokes may end up uneven or out of alignment, the brakes may not work properly as a result, and so on.

Conversely, if the hub is good and working properly, but the spokes are bent, or loose, then the rim will be out of round; we refer to a good round rim as being "true." Your son's life is no different. If the hub, or the core of his life, is effective and working properly, and if the spokes, or the individual areas of your son's life, are good and the wheel true, he has a significantly higher probability of having a quality life, one that he and you can both be proud of and enjoy. If on the other hand, there is a problem with the wheel, your son will struggle, sometimes dramatically, with the quality of his life, and you will have to go along for the ride. Let's look at each of these two components a little more closely.

THE HUB

As a kid working on your bike, or a father working on your kids' bikes, you know the hub is important, but you don't give much thought to it. You just assume, hope, or trust that it is put together well and it's working. Yet it's the most important and most complicated part. If there is something wrong with most components of a wheel, you can fix them. A bent or broken spoke, you can replace. A hole in a tire or tube, you can repair. Brakes not working, you can adjust them. Gears not shifting right, you can adjust them. But if the hub comes apart on us, or isn't working properly, we're done. We either have to take it to a professional for repair, or we just toss the wheel and buy a whole new one. The hub is what allows the wheel to turn well, or at all. The hub is what the spokes are anchored to as they extend out to the rim. The hub is where most modern-day bikes have the disc brakes attached. The hub is what the gears are attached to that give us speed and momentum and propel us, or resistance to help slow us down. The entire form and function of the wheel are affected by the quality and condition of the hub. The wheel is enabled or impeded by the hub.

THE SPOKES

An out-of-round rim creates all kinds of problems. As boys, we knew riding a bike with a bent rim, or one out of round, was difficult, if not impossible. Remember when you used to spin your rim and watch it wobble back and forth? You knew it was out of round. In the bike world, your wheel was no longer "true." A "true" wheel was a perfect, or near perfect, round wheel that rolled straight. This was really important. If it wasn't "true," it would rub on the brakes in that spot and slow you down. Or remember when you bent or broke a spoke, and that part of the wheel could bend when you hit it on a curb or went off a jump? The strength of your wheel was suddenly and dramatically affected. We weren't going anywhere very fast, or without a lot of effort, with a bent rim, and we weren't doing many tricks or riding hard with bent or broken spokes. My younger son, Brendan, is a skateboarder, and he understands the concept through the idea of a flat spot on his skateboard wheel. A flat spot on his skateboard wheel severely hinders the board and his performance. The spokes of a bicycle also determine the size of the wheel, whether it's a 15-inch, 21-inch, or 27-inch one. We also know that the bigger the wheel, the less rotation and energy necessary to cover the same distance. The spokes, like the hub, matter significantly to the quality of your son's life.

CONNECTING THE WHEEL AND THE RITE OF PASSAGE

Here is the corollary between a bicycle wheel and your son's Rite of Passage. Your son's Rite of Passage must be holistic in order for it to be of real and true value to him in this modern and complex time. I believe that from my experience, the myriad of statistics we read and hear about, and our own observations, too many fathers are either not interested or not focused on raising their sons well, or they are focused on the peripherals (the tube, the tire, etc.) and missing the essentials: the hub and the spokes. They are dealing with the symptoms, and not addressing the root cause. Our sons, your son, need a good solid hub to which the spokes of his life, the areas of his life, are anchored.

He needs to have spokes that are straight and equally extended so that the wheel, his life, is true and rolls well. The illustration that follows is what I believe are the principles, or the components, of a great Rite of Passage, in the form of a wheel. Faith represents the hub of the wheel. It is the core of my life; everything that I value stems from, and is influenced by, my faith. Faith as the hub may be obvious to some readers, but not so obvious to others. My reasons for making faith the hub will be explained in the next chapter. The remaining components are the spokes: character & integrity, direction (values, vision, and goals), chivalry, sexual integrity, people (how to deal with them), money, work (as in ethics), and the stretch. These spokes represent each area of my life, and of the men I observe and council, that are essential for developing a good, quality life that spins "true," creates the least amount of resistance, the greatest amount of positive momentum, and gets the best performance results.

THINGS TO CONSIDER ABOUT THE WHEEL AND YOUR SON

- Is the hub good? If your son's faith is solidified, then you have something firm and sure to anchor the spokes to – a great start!

- Is the wheel "true?" Are all the spokes evenly developed? If he's knocking it out of the park in the money area and that spoke is growing well, but he's completely blowing it with sexual integrity, that wheel isn't going anywhere. It's coming to a screeching halt.

- Is your son running on a 15" or 27" wheel? Develop each area of your son's life fully so that he produces the best, quality life with the least amount of energy, and gets there in the shortest amount of time.

- You can't ignore the wheel. Anyone who has had a bike knows that it requires attention, maintenance, and tune-ups in order to perform consistently well. And if you maintain the wheel, it will last a very long time, relatively trouble free. Conversely, ignoring its care and maintenance will leave you stranded on the trail or on the side of the road, oftentimes injured.

At the risk of stretching this analogy a little too far, let me say that just because your son may have a solid, true, 27-inch wheel doesn't mean he isn't going to hit some bumps in the road. Bumps happen; that's life. However, your son's ability to overcome those bumps in the road, that is, the obstacles life will throw at him, without him being completely sidelined is significantly increased. More importantly, with proper training, motivation, and vision for a great future, he will be able to avoid the major bumps, and be diverted from truly catastrophic, long-term, detrimental mistakes. A rite of passage is not about your sons having trouble free lives. There's no such thing. It's about preparing your sons not to be the cause of the trouble in their lives. So let's not be "Ready, Fire, Aim" fathers. Let's be "Ready, Aim, Fire" fathers.

PERSONAL ASSESSMENT

Before you begin to unpack the core principles, the spokes of the wheel, I believe it is important in the "Ready" stage of "Ready, Aim, Fire" that we look at ourselves closely. Therefore, following each chapter, there is a personal assessment section. Each spoke will be accompanied by an opportunity for self-assessment. This is a critical component in conducting your son's rite of passage. What follows is my suggested outline of an assessment model.

If you have the accompanying Father's Planner, in each spoke of your rite of passage there is a personal assessment for you to make. This is a four-step process:

1. The inventory of where you are personally.
2. What do you have to teach your son, either from doing it well or doing it wrong?
3. What, if any, personal adjustments do you need to make to model well for your son?
4. What resources do you need to equip your son (and maybe yourself) for this spoke?

Step 1 – Inventory where you are personally.

I have borrowed a simple measurement system from my pastor, Roger Archer. It's a baseball metaphor, but it works. It's called Home Run, Base Hit, or Strike Out. I encourage you to consider where you are today in regard to each spoke of the wheel. I will use finances as an example of what I am talking about with regard to assessment:

Home Run – You have knocked it out of the park, good. If its finances and you have done a great job in this area: you tithe faithfully, if you're a Christian; you are generous; you have saved diligently and prepared for the unexpected; you have set up retirement; you live on a budget, exercise self-control, and keep your family within those boundaries, etc. You have hit a home run.

Base Hit – You're doing OK, but there is work to do. By this I mean you are working toward good financial disciplines, but you have a tendency to fall back into undisciplined behavior. You don't have the strength to tell your family "no" when necessary. You have not consistently given to others. You may be making it on your paycheck, but you're not consistently saving and accumulating to take care of your family's future needs.

Strike out – You're really not doing well at all. You are living from paycheck to paycheck. There is no discipline or restraint in you or your family's spending; you have no concept or, or even attempt to, budget to live within your means. You don't like living this way, but you haven't changed your habits.

<u>Step 2 – What do you have to teach your son, either from doing it well or doing it wrong?</u>

After taking an inventory, you may be like I was; I had some areas of strength from which I could teach my sons. I also had some areas of weakness where I needed to improve, and I could teach my sons what not to do by my example, and learn and grow with them. Teach from your areas of strength, and use your mistakes or areas of weakness as illustrations as you learn together. Your mistakes and missteps are oftentimes very powerful teaching tools, as long as you have recovered, or are actively showing your son strength and perseverance and discipline to grow.

<u>Step 3 – What, if any, personal adjustments do you need to make to model well for your son?</u>

If you're not hitting a home run in any of the spokes, what

adjustments do you need to make in your life? Your life and lessons are better "caught" than "taught" with people. Your boys will be hypersensitive to hypocrisy and double standards. You will lose all credibility with them, and others, if you are not authentic, vulnerable, and honest. If you have not done so well financially, don't tell and teach your son to do something you are not willing to do yourself. If there is any area that you feel ill-equipped to teach your son, get over it! Show him what not to do by the example of your life, and teach him and yourself how to do it right. If it's finances, then go to a financial management class together, learn and utilize budgeting together, work on debt elimination together. Learn to say "no" together.

Step 4 – What resources do you need to equip your son (and maybe yourself) for this spoke?

If you are hitting a home run, find a resource that you can go through together, for example, a familiar book on good financial management principles through which you can take your son. You will have your own example to support the model. If you are not doing so well in this spoke, find a resource, and maybe a mentor, to learn together with your son. One excellent example is *Financial Peace University* with Dave Ramsey. This is an extremely solid and practical video-based class from which you will personally gain much, and by which your son will get rock solid principles to operate.

Ready to get started? As we begin to construct this wheel, we must start with the core, or the hub. In my case, this is incontrovertibly my faith. Let's get started.

FIVE

THE HUB: FAITH
WHAT DO YOU BELIEVE?

A faith is a necessity to a man. Woe to him who believes in nothing.

– Victor Hugo

FAITH OR NO FAITH – THAT IS NOT THE QUESTION

First and foremost for me in this journey is faith. It is inexorably linked to who I am, what I do, and why I do it. This may not be the case for you. Now, before you close the book, let me ask you a question: Where does your definition of a man come from? If you are like me, you never had a clear definition. I had a vague idea from watching other men and viewing popular media – but no clear definition was given to me intentionally. I suspect this may be true for you, as well, and most likely for our fathers. So we morph into something that is a counterfeit of a real man.

I did not set out to write a religious book, or one overtly Christian. I did not want to exclude someone from the process of equipping his son because he is not a Christian. But I must be honest with the reader and true to myself. This is a book about fathers and sons, and more to the point, about *this* father and *his* sons. My story includes my faith – my faith in God, and specifically as a Christian, in Jesus Christ. As I mentioned previously, I came into a relationship with God late in life at 32 years old, and it radically transformed me. In fact, the only reason you are reading this book is because of that experience and the subsequent changes in my attitudes since then. More to the point, it is the only reason that I know what the true and authentic definition of a man is.

Consequently, it's impossible for me to write this book and attempt to straddle some gap between a faith-based, biblical view of life, and a non-biblical view of life. I hope that if you are reading this book and you are not a Christian you will have the courage and love for your son to stay with it. Who knows where you'll end up?

You may be saying to yourself that faith doesn't matter so much. But having lived on both sides of the issue for long enough to experience the differences, I would argue passionately against that attitude. Everyone has a worldview. Your worldview is what you believe in, how you make sense of things, what influences your actions and decisions, and, truthfully, everyone believes in something.

At the most basic level, everyone falls into one of two categories. Either you believe in, and put your faith in, a scientific theory about a massive cosmic explosion that then randomly reorganized itself into order (evolution), or you believe in, and put your faith in, a creator who put all this together (creation or intelligent design). You see, you are ultimately exercising faith regardless of which belief system you have chosen. I say "chosen," but in reality for most, we didn't really choose. We were influenced strongly by parents, teachers, pastors, the media, and so on, early and often in our lives, and unbeknownst to us, we unconsciously formed a worldview. Some of us (very few) mature to the point where we begin to undertake serious inquiry; we allow our belief system to be questioned, challenged, and tested, and we ultimately make a conscious decision about what we believe.

If you are in the first category, your faith is hinged to scientists' ever-expanding theory based on what they may or may not discover. For example, there was a planet Pluto, and now there is not. I am not down on science; it is extraordinarily useful and good. I love to read about it, I am fascinated by many scientific discoveries, and I'm thankful for many of those discoveries; the quality of my life is infinitely better because of science. In my opinion, it is a great discipline that serves man well. But it is not what I base my existence on any longer, or subsequently, how I see and order my life.

Now, if you are in the second category (creation), you may simply stay at that basic level of believing in some force that takes several religious tangents, or you may transcend to the next level of discovery, a Creator, and that creator is God. You have moved from an "it" to a "who." At that point your worldview gets more specifically defined and focused. The next level of discovery for this group is who the "who" actually is: a toymaker that wound it up and is letting it run down? Or is he personally interested in and involved in his creation? This takes us to the next level of discovery for the second group - Christianity. It's important that Christian faith is further defined. It's the ultimate acknowledgement and acceptance of the profound love of a creator, God, who loved the world (you and me) so much so, that he gave his one and only Son so that everyone who believes in him, Jesus Christ, to restore us to the original intended relationship with God, will not perish but have eternal life (John 3:16). Now, even if you don't believe that, stick with me for a moment.

My Christian faith provides a worldview that puts everything in the context of a Creator who loves you and me. He created us and he has a purpose for our individual existence. Everything that we see, feel, and touch, and that which we do not see or feel or touch, he created for our good. There was an original intention by God for a world void of sin, debauchery, death, decay, pain, suffering, and the like. However, because he made us free moral agents, a decision was made and an action taken that opened the door for a corruptive force to enter into creation and produce the decaying, debased world we experience today. The decaying and debasing nature of things now includes us humans, our mind, body, soul, and spirit, as well as the rest of creation.

It is that decay or corruption, particularly of our mind and spirit, that has caused us to even deny the existence or authority of a creator. When we do that, reject a creator, and by extension his original order, plan, and design for our lives, and his power to assist us, we by default choose the opposite of that. We become our own little gods unto ourselves, deciding for ourselves what is right, moral, good, bad, and so on. You may be familiar with the term "free radicals." These are molecules in our bodies that are very unstable, and they are largely responsible for causing tissue damage and disease in our bodies. Antioxidants, on the other hand, are molecules that prevent free radicals from doing damage and facilitate health. When we have a worldview devoid of God, we are free radicals. Conversely, a worldview based on a faith in God introduces antioxidants into our life and helps prevent us from damaging ourselves, others, and the rest of creation.

Furthermore, to draw from chemistry for another example, what we don't understand in that state of mind, one void of a worldview based on faith in God, is that we are missing the key building block that makes everything else work properly. The cells of your body are, in part, made up of chromosomes. If the chromosomes are healthy, your cells are healthy and you are relatively free from defects. If, however, one of your chromosomes is missing or flawed, your entire body is affected and changed. To have a worldview other than one influenced and shaped by a faith in God is to have a worldview that is missing a chromosome, which adversely affects the entirety of your life and the way you see the world. And interestingly enough, if a person has a defect and he or she is surrounded by a bunch of people who all have the same defect, do they even know they have a defect? No, they do not. It takes the introduction of someone healthy to cause the others to even ask the question, "Is there something not quite right with me?"

THE FORMATION OF MY ATTITUDES

I grew up without any specific emphasis on faith in God, and, consequently, with an absence in any strong core set of values, principles, or morals; I was a free radical. I grew up like a lot of people, with a general and often distorted sense of right and wrong.

My parents would occasionally go to church at the traditional times of year: Christmas and Easter. Every once in a while they would go because they thought it was the right thing to do, and so we'd go to church a few Sundays a year. In all fairness to them, that is my perception. But at the end of the day, it was not brought to bear in any real, significant, or memorable way.

It's also pretty interesting how important it was to get married in a church, when my wife and I could not have cared less about God under any other circumstance. However, like many other people, I saw an enormous gap in what religious people said about how we should act and what I saw the same people actually doing, not to mention what I saw non-religious people doing, such as my parents. So for me, religion had no value. And in my world, the concept of an actual relationship with God didn't exist.

Like most kids, I saw people going to church to appease their conscience, and if that's you, I'm not writing this to make you feel bad or think disrespectfully or disparagingly about yourself or your parents; it's just how it was for me, and how it is for a lot of people and families. That kind of "religious" activity does not produce a faith or a relationship like the one I have experienced. My experience raises the subject of faith to the paramount position of the hub of my wheel, the thing to which all my spokes are anchored. I would encourage you to read through this chapter, even if your inclination is to pass it over. I am not trying to "convert" anyone to Christianity, only to share my experience because of its relevance in my life. You might find we have some things in common.

Religious or not, Christian or not, the Bible is an absolutely brilliant guide, or manual, for life. And that is the truth. You read earlier about the way I lived my life, and the consequences of all that. I have come to understand that the Bible describes and exactly predicts those outcomes; it's scary how accurate it is. Most of my life I had rejected the Bible and its principles and truths, as well as a relationship with God, because I believed erroneously that I would have to live under all these rules and regulations; I thought my existence wouldn't be any fun. In retrospect, that was ignorance. I was rejecting something that I didn't really understand.

The attitudes I had developed about the Bible and God were really based on other people's attitudes, those who didn't know any more than I did. But it was easier to believe them and do what I wanted rather than to discover anything for myself. This might even describe you. If so, I encourage you to dig in a little bit and do some honest investigation of your own, and get outside of the group you have always been with that holds those same old attitudes. You might be surprised at what you find.

The reason faith is core for me is because after I discovered the truth about God, began to order my life differently, and submitted to his plan for living life I began to experience radical changes for the positive. My life was completely transformed, and it didn't take long before I realized that the true way to freedom, joy, peace, and purpose was found inside the boundaries that God defines.

BOWLING WITH GOD

It's kind of like bumper bowling. When you were little, or if you have kids and you go bowling, sometimes the bowling alley will put up bumpers along the lanes so the ball doesn't go into the gutter. Well, to put it simply, my life before God was like bowling without bumpers, and I spent a lot of my time in the gutter; I just didn't realize it. This was in large part because the people I ran with were in the same position, so it seemed normal. I just knew that I didn't enjoy much of it, and I sure didn't like the end result of a lot of it. My bowling score for life was a 79 out of a possible 300 – a pretty dismal one! When I discovered who God is and started living and ordering my life according to His instructions in the Bible, it was as if, suddenly, the bumpers came up and I was staying out of the gutter! I might not have been scoring a 300 perfect game, but I was scoring much higher than before, and there were no gutter balls or empty frames. It was awesome!

What makes me so passionate about this? It is simple – compare and contrast. I had lived 32 years without the bumpers, and I knew what that produced in my life. I had only lived a short time of my life with the bumpers up, and it was already awesome. If I could help my boys avoid the kind of life I had lived, without the drugs, alcohol, sex, pornography, bad relationships, financial disasters, and so on, why wouldn't I?

When I found myself staying "in the lane," everything in life began to improve: relationships, finances, career, outlook on life, attitudes, you name it. My marriage was restored, I got my family back, I got a rewarding career, I found a whole new world of things to enjoy, and I began to experience a truly fulfilling life abounding with, dare I say it…fun and joy and a real, authentic peace. That's not to say that I didn't have difficult times or challenges; I had plenty. Granted, they were all consequences of my own choices, but the hope I now had that I could turn these things around in my life was enormous.

Faith in God, which led me to the word of God, the Bible, had completely reshaped my attitudes and thinking. Faith had literally changed the way I viewed my life. It was no longer so much about me, but what comes after me. I was excited at the idea that I could have a chance to shape and influence my boys' lives, and, consequently, their families and the generations that would follow from my lineage. All of a sudden, I was thinking and talking about "legacy." I began to think about 10, 20, 30 years from now, and not just about myself, but my family. Think about it for a minute. If you have discovered something really cool to give to your children or a friend, and you knew how beneficial it would be, wouldn't you share it with them? Remember when you were a teenager and you discovered a great new band? You couldn't wait to tell everyone you knew. It was like that for me, except it was much more significant than a new favorite band. I wasn't holding this back from anyone, especially my sons.

How many of us, and by extension our families, have had detours in our lives because we lacked the knowledge, training, vision, and hope that faith in God provides? How many of you have had those unexpected occurrences that pulled your life out of the lane and into the gutter, things that were, in hindsight, completely avoidable?

THE REST OF MY STORY

A life of faith is like bowling in another way. In bowling, you get better over time as you learn and practice. You will have a good game, and then a not-so-good game. But gradually, over time, your good games come more and more frequently, and you have fewer and fewer bad games. Over time your "average" improves. You have to look at your life of faith as a whole, not only in part. I say this because, in spite of the radical changes in my life that began in March of 1996, my wife justifiably left and ultimately divorced me (for the second time, if you're paying attention). The heartbreak and agony I was experiencing were difficult. I had messed things up so badly, but I had also finally figured some things out and began to change. I was developing a whole new understanding, passion, and responsibility as a husband and a father, but it appeared that it was all too late. I was scared to death that I had lost my chance to create change in my family tree with my wife and boys, and I had lost my chance to right my wrongs and pass along a better legacy to the next generation. I feared my window had closed and I had missed the opportunity altogether to help my boys avoid the life that I had experienced.

To make a long story short, I was granted another (or third) chance. Nearly two years after my wife had me, she had her own personal encounter with God and came to faith in Jesus Christ. Subsequently, God in his grace and power restored our relationship and marriage. We were remarried for the third, and final, time on June 13, 1998. It is very emotional for me as I write about this so many years later, because I had been afforded another chance! That is why I have held this part of my story for this section of the book. This would not have happened had it not been for my faith.

That is not to say that, if my wife and I hadn't gotten back together, I would not have had an opportunity to powerfully influence my boys. I was already working hard to change my situation; I had gotten a new job that allowed me to move closer in order to have as much exposure and influence as possible. I wasn't going to quit just because I was divorced. But I thank God for the tremendous opportunity I have received to do it all over and change the legacy of my family, not only for my sons, but also for the generations to come. I truly believe that by changing my life, and my sons' lives, we could have the potential to change our entire family legacy, and maybe even the culture.

The reality is that the rest of life doesn't make much sense if it is not built on the foundation of a faith in God. It's like building a skyscraper: if the foundation isn't square, you might not notice it on the 1st, 2nd, 3rd, or 4th floor, but by the 6th or 7th floor nothing fits right. Doors don't fit or close, windows don't fit, the walls aren't square; that whole building is a mess. That was my life. But my faith in God, and adhering to his instructions, was the starting point in my turn around. So for my sons, it had to start with the foundation of faith. Everything I share is really rooted in my expanding understanding of God's best intentions for people. From there, the principles of values, vision, goals, integrity, character, women, sex, relationships, money, work, and adventure all come together in a context that produces a life that is well lived and produces a legacy that is worth writing about. Let's teach our sons to bowl.

TEACHING MY SONS TO BOWL

I had an additional epiphany in 1996 as I recognized that I had a chance to raise my boys to live their lives correctly from the start, to teach them how to bowl. After all, they were only one and three. If I did this well, they would not have to go through all the misery and consequences of making such poor choices as I had done. They could live a life without regret, without the life-altering bad decisions that I had made. It took me an additional 10 years to get from my epiphany in 1996 to my process in 2006. What did I know about doing this thing right in 1996? Not much, but I had spent ten years learning and practicing, improving my average. Where I had been thoughtful about raising my boys in a faith in God, I was not as intentional and purposeful as I could, or should, have been. I had raised them in the faith, to personally know God, through Jesus Christ, which is the difference between religion and relationship. They had been grounded in the word of God. But it was time to go to the next level.

As my boys begin their rites of passage, the first place we start in constructing this wheel is the hub…faith. We spend our first couple of months in this area. Since they have a foundation in their faith in God, my responsibility is now to help them own their faith as theirs. It is way too easy for a child's faith simply to be an extension of their parents, just because. But that is a precarious place for your son to be. He has to have some decent fundamental apologetics – that is, simply knowing what he believes, and why he believes it.

I explain to my sons why this area is so important, and I use my life as a graphic illustration. We spend a fair amount of time comparing and contrasting; my boys learn a lot about my life at this point – the good, the bad, and the ugly. Mostly the bad and the ugly; the good comes always as the contrast. My goal is that they would come to understand both the power of their personal relationship with God, and the power of the application of His Word to their lives. This would be an outgrowth of their personal confidence in the validity and integrity of the Bible and Jesus Christ. I take them through a book that I have chosen, *A Case for Christ* by Lee Strobel[1], the Book of Proverbs in the Bible, and other specific passages in the Bible. This helps them understand the "what" and the "why" for their faith.

It is important to me at this stage in their lives that they own their own faith and don't simply have the faith that I have. That might have been adequate and acceptable up to this point, but from here forward they are 100% accountable for what they believe and why. If they don't take this step, then it will be too easy for someone later on to come along and derail them. This is the time they make the personal discovery of the power of a life lived "in the lane." I want my sons to stand on their own two feet, to own their faith, and be able to defend it.

We talk about all the challenges of faith, the perceived challenges to the Bible that people who don't really know what they are talking about will throw at them. I know these people; I used to be one of them. This isn't a "do as I say" lecture. This is a serious inquiry into the fundamental principles and truths that underpin their faith. I encourage them to ask the tough questions. There is no question they can't ask, and there is nothing off limits or taboo. I encourage them to talk about it all, to get it all out and do the hard work of learning, discovering, and developing their own beliefs that will guide and shape their lives, and the lives of their future children. It is through this process that they will develop their worldview, which will ultimately shape their attitudes and values, and strongly influence their actions and decisions.

I also live my life of faith out in the open with my boys. They see that, as a Christian, I am not perfect, but they also see that I am not a hypocrite or a "poser." I am authentic, I am a flawed man living out my faith in real time in front of real people, and it's genuine, albeit imperfect. My boys don't see a contradiction in my life at church, with other Christians, or in any other environment. And if they do, they have my permission and encouragement to call me on it. And they have! The stakes are too high for them to dismiss this critical core because of my failure or hypocrisy.

If you read through this chapter and you are a Christian, you can relate to what I experienced. If you are not a Christian, you may be able to relate to the first part of my life. As for what you do with the rest of your life, well, that is a decision for you to make. I hope you choose well; there is an amazing adventure and experience waiting for you! I would encourage you to find a local church and talk to a pastor. It may seem a little scary, it was for me, but pastors are normal people like you. Remember, I am one now, and most pastors are a pretty understanding group. At a minimum, I would encourage you to begin by reading *A Case for Christ* by Lee Strobel; it might be a great place for you to begin your own process of discovery.

With faith as the backdrop, let's move on to vision, values, and goals. I won't be going back into the roots of my faith; just know that it's the lens through which I see everything.

PERSONAL ASSESSMENT – THE HUB: FAITH

1. Take an inventory of where you are personally.
   - Home Run – Why? What evidence is there?
   - Base Hit – Why? What evidence is there?
   - Strike Out – Why? What evidence is there?

2. What do you have to teach your son, either from doing it well or doing it wrong?
   - Where have you been successful and what can you teach your son?
   - Where have you missed and what can you teach your son about it (what have you learned)?

3. What, if any, personal adjustments do you need to make to model well for your son?
   - As you assess your life currently against the hub, what needs to change in your life in order for you to have integrity with yourself and your son as you teach him to live well in the hub?

4. What resources do you need to equip your son in this area that either reinforce your success, or may augment where you may be lacking personally?
   - Search out resources and teaching tools: books, classes, videos, seminars, mentors, etc., that either help illustrate and support your strength here, or augment your weakness and create a strength in both you and your son.

Tip: Maybe this is just as simple as beginning to go to church together every week, or if you're already there, spending one day a week in the morning for a few minutes together reading the Bible and talking about what you are reading. Maybe it's you and your son sitting together once a week in a men's group with more mature men in the faith who can teach both you and your son. On the other hand, maybe this is a big leap for you because you have not made a thoughtful, deductive decision about your own faith. Your beliefs were transferred and acquired by osmosis from others without real analysis and reflection. Consequently, like many who are misinformed as I was, you either don't believe in God, or you believe in some generic and unengaged God different from the God of the Bible. For you, maybe the first step is asking yourself the questions about why you believe what you believe, getting outside your comfort zone and reading A Case For Christ *yourself, or talking to someone who professes a strong faith in God and Jesus Christ. Maybe for you, you need to establish your hub.*

1st SPOKE: CHARACTER & INTEGRITY
WHAT'S IN A NAME?

Character is much easier kept than recovered.

– Thomas Paine

Have the courage to say no. Have the courage to face the truth. Do the right thing because it is right. These are the magic keys to living your life with integrity.

– W. Clement Stone

WHAT'S IN A NAME?

This may not be the first time you've heard the question, asked the question, or answered the question, "What's in a name"? Or just maybe it is. This is a very important question for a young man. Our names – his name, your name, my name – means something specific to everyone who knows us. Why is it so important to your emerging man? *Association.* That's right, association.

Every human being makes associations in his or her mind; it's the way we are wired. We hear a word, and our minds create a picture. That picture is associated with our experience, and there is a corresponding emotion that influences our actions and decisions. Let me give you an example. I say, "Starbucks." Your mind creates an image. For many of you, when I say Starbucks you see the green and white logo, or maybe your favorite drink, or maybe you see the front of your favorite Starbucks. If you have had positive experiences with Starbucks, you have a positive association and a positive emotional response.

Conversely, maybe you have had negative experiences with Starbucks, or you have some negative feelings about the organization for some reason. If so, when I say, "Starbucks," your mind goes through the same process of the image and the association, but your association and corresponding response is negative. So, if you like Starbucks, you say to me, *"I love Starbucks."* If you don't like Starbucks, you say to me, *"I can't stand Starbucks."*

What does this have to do with your son's name? The process of the mind associating has another very important powerful connection, that of belief. These associations, the accumulation of experiences, form your beliefs about an individual, a thing such as a restaurant, or an institution, such as the church, and so on. Your belief is your "truth" about that person, place, or thing. The same is true with our names. Your son's name will mean something to everyone who knows him. Whatever their experience is with your son will determine what people think and say about him. It will be their belief about your son, their "truth" about your son.

The questions you want to ask your son are these: What do you want people to say, how do you want them to feel, and what do you want them to think when they hear your name? What do you want their belief, their "truth," to be about you? Let's put it another way. Two people are talking to each other. One has known you for a while and the other person just met you. The person who just met you mentions to the other that he just met you. What do you want the other person to say about you? Do you want him to say, *"Oh, Allen is awesome; I love that guy! He's one of the most consistent and trustworthy guys I know. I can always count on him, and he always seems positive."* Or do you want the response to be, *"Allen Jones. Yeah, I know him. Whatever you do, don't put yourself in a position where you have to depend on him; he's not the most consistent guy. He's also kind of negative, kind of a pessimist."*

Not very many people consciously think about name association as adults, and I guarantee you hardly any young men are considering this. But this is no less than a person's reputation we are talking about, and as we know, our reputation often precedes us. Our name and what people think of us are linked.

The great question for your son is: When someone says your name, what do you want your name to mean? This strikes right at the core of a man. It speaks of his character, his integrity, his attitudes, and his convictions. You obviously can't control what others think or say, but you can conduct yourself in such a way that makes it difficult for people to have a negative association with your name, securing your reputation and the quality of your name.

CHARACTER & INTEGRITY

These two words are complementary, although they are not synonymous. Most people have come to use the two words together as if the were one word, or they use one words to describe the other. That is understandable when you read the definitions of the two:

Character: The aggregate of features and traits that form the individual nature of some person or thing; reputation.

Integrity: Firm adherence to a code of especially moral values – incorruptibility; an unimpaired condition – soundness; the quality or state of being complete or undivided – completeness.

When we break them down, however, and look at them more closely, we see they have different concepts. Conceptually, character is an overall holistic description of a person, "the aggregate of features and traits that form the individual nature." However, it doesn't automatically assign the *quality* of character, such as a good or bad character. Integrity, on the other hand, implies the *quality* of a person, "moral values; incorruptibility; an unimpaired condition." The two combined complement and define each other. I won't spend much time trying to untangle them, but rather talk about how the two intertwined and used together give meaning.

As a society, we have implied and attached meaning to these words character and integrity. We generally use these words to say something favorable of someone. For example, when we say, "He has character," we are admiring that person's overall behaviors, actions, and lifestyle. We don't generally say he has a "bad character." Instead, we use other words, such as "he's a cheat," "he's a liar," "he's unreliable," or "he's unfaithful."

The same is true when we talk about a person's integrity; we will generally use the word to describe someone favorably. Let's say we observe an individual choosing a hard path with negative consequences over an easy way out, for example, telling the truth when he could have lied and gotten away with something. We would say, "He has integrity." If we think someone lacks integrity, we would say that he is duplicitous, a liar, or a cheat. You can see how the two words become jumbled up and intertwined.

The two words character and integrity are like the word "consequence." We have come to use this word generally to mean something negative. When we say to our kids, "There will be consequences," we nearly always mean negative ones, and so the assignment of the negative is connoted in the word. However, the word, in fact, is neutral.

The words character and integrity, generally, imply something favorable in our culture. So rather than fight upstream against the current, let's go with the flow in incorporating the two terms into one coherent statement that implies something favorable. We want to think of the words like this:

Character and integrity come together to describe the overall quality, consistency, and continuity in a man's life. The aggregate of an individual man's life is a firm adherence to his core beliefs, acted upon in a consistent manner that produce a continuity in his words and his actions, that produce a life worth modeling and a good reputation.

WHERE ARE CHARACTER & INTEGRITY HIDING?

If you have seen *Gladiator*, what comes to mind when I say "Maximus Decimus Meridius" (Russell Crowe's character)? If you have seen *Braveheart*, what comes to mind when I say, "William Wallace" (Mel Gibson's character)? If you have seen the movie *Lord of The Rings*, what comes to mind when I say, "Aragorn" (Viggo

Mortensen's character)? You get the idea. Each of these characters leaves an indelible impression in your mind and your heart. You are moved by their lives, and what they stand for. You don't even have to remember great detail; all you have to do is think of the character in the movie or hear his name and you are inspired. This has been the case for every man throughout time. There is something that moves us when we see inspirational, noble, valiant men of quality that inspire us, even if only for the moment, to be better versions of ourselves. Maximus was famous for saying "strength and honor." William Wallace was famous for saying "They can take our life, but they can't take our freedom." Aragorn was famous for saying "If by my life or death I can protect you, I will. You have my sword..."

Then there is the movie called *Act of Valor*. Just watching this movie – the heroism and selflessness of its characters – inspires you and moves you, and causes you to want to be those kind of men. The movie ends with the reading of a poem by Chief Tecumseh. Google it, read it, and see if it doesn't do something in the deepest part of your soul. There is something in the heart of a man that makes him long to be a man of character; he longs to have his name mean something significant and noble. We all want to have our "strength and honor" associations, and that is a good thing. I suggest to you that where this once was a man's conscious goal, and a father's concern for his son, generally speaking, this has been laid to rest in our society's consciousness. But I tell you, it is not dead, only dormant in the hearts of men. In our culture, it can be resuscitated and made vital again, one young man at a time.

Fortunately, we don't have to look only to movie characters for our inspiration for having a quality name. Do any of these names ring a bell: George Washington, Abraham Lincoln, Martin Luther King, Jr., Winston Churchill? There are many historical figures that are real and memorable that can inspire our young men to have character and integrity, and a great name. As you look around, there are some men in your life – maybe close, maybe at more of a distance – to show your boys. Make no mistake, though; when you look at the leaders and role models today, it is getting increasingly difficult to find great examples to show your sons.

How your boys live their lives out each day will determine the quality of their names. If you can get them to understand this principle, then you will go a long way in laying the foundation for the rest of your work with them. Think about it. What things impact the quality of your name more than faith, values, character, finances, how you treat women and conduct yourself in relationships, and your work?

We learn most effectively when we are able to compare and contrast. Your responsibility is to compare and contrast for them the legacy and product of different people's lives that have guarded or discarded the quality of their names. This is not difficult if you look at history, politics, and the family. You will see plenty of examples of both. You may even want to consider the quality of your own name. Maybe there was a day when the quality of your name wasn't so impressive, but today you are highly regarded for all the right reasons. Your own example is important, and a great lesson in character and integrity themselves. Although this may not need to be stated, be aware that it is important to do this in a way that is not degrading to the people you use as an example. Make sure that any examples you use are contemporary enough, or significant enough in history that your sons can relate.

Because my sons were old enough (13 and 15 at the time), I was able to use Bill Clinton as an example. His conduct in office as the President of the United States severely damaged the quality of his name, both his conduct with women in the White House, and the subsequent attempts to skirt (no pun intended) around the truth and lie about it. This is not political, by the way; a similar and extreme lack of character and integrity is seen in the example of Richard Nixon. He cheated and lied in office, and forever tarnished his name. There are plenty of current events to choose from. Unfortunately, there is no shortage of men in positions of power and influence who will sell themselves out and provide lots of examples, with plenty of negative consequences, to make the case.

Not surprisingly, this is one of the areas most viciously attacked, as our culture essentially says a person's character and integrity are irrelevant. Our sons hear this message loud and clear, as corporate leaders, sports figures, media figures, and politicians who are running and representing our country get a pass for their behavior. We give these people great accolades, and I have even seen the words "character" or "integrity" used alongside their names, knowing full well that by a stricter definition from only a few decades ago, they would not have had those validating words put anywhere near their names.

When your son applies for his first job and they call for references, what will these people say? When your son meets his future wife and she talks to people who know him, what will they say? When he gets his first chance at a real promotion, what will his peers and superiors say? When his days have been numbered, and he is eulogized, what will his family and friends say?

This is one of the first and most important steps in living life on purpose. Character and integrity are not exclusively assigned to men of faith. We see men who do not have a firm conviction or adherence to a faith in God who have learned the value of these qualities. We also see men who profess a faith in God, but their lack of character and integrity both ruin their reputation and also impugn the reputations of the church and of God. But these are generally the exception rather than the norm, as you see men of good, strong character and integrity. If you dig deep enough, you will usually find that these men inherited character and integrity from someone who had an understanding of God and his Word, either from their own life experience, or from having it passed down to them by someone who did.

It used to be so embedded in our identity as a nation that the Bible influenced everything we created and did: our laws, our standards, and our national ethics. So there is no way for me, with integrity (there is that word, uncorrupted and unimpaired), to rightly teach my boys about character and integrity without the Bible. While we talk about my life, other people, and character, we also spend time in the Book of Proverbs and other parts of Scripture to find the truth and value of these foundational qualities.

Here are just a few examples:

- *"Have you noticed my servant Job? He is the finest man in all the earth. He is blameless—a man of complete integrity. He fears God and stays away from evil."* (Job, chapter 1, vs. 8)
- *"To the faithful you (God) show yourself faithful; to those with integrity you show integrity."* (Psalms, chapter 18, vs. 25)
- *"The LORD detests people with crooked hearts, but he delights in those with integrity."* (Proverbs, chapter 11, vs. 20)
- *"Bad company corrupts good character."* (1 Corinthians, chapter 15, vs. 33)
- *"Choose a good reputation over great riches; being held in high esteem is better than silver or gold."* (Proverbs, chapter 22, vs. 1)
- *"So an elder must be a man whose life is above reproach. He must be faithful to his wife. He must exercise self-control, live wisely, and have a good reputation."* (1 Timothy, chapter 3, vs. 2)

- *"The LORD curses the house of the wicked, but he blesses the home of the upright."* (Proverbs, chapter 3, vs. 33)

If you are honest with yourself, you don't have to be a Christian to understand the wisdom and benefit of the previous passages.

As it relates to my sons, I was able to use my life as a great example of what it looks like to be lacking in character and integrity, and fortunately, of what it looks like to live a life that contains much character and integrity. I'm not suggesting that I'm the perfect model; most certainly, I'm not. But by God's grace, and my decision to live a different life and apply God's word to my life, my life has become a much better model.

As you have read, prior to the age of 32 my life was anything but a good model. I didn't care about my reputation in regards to the things that really matter; I didn't care about my legacy. I certainly was not interested in doing anything that might have made my life more challenging, like telling the truth, or being disciplined in my spending, for example. The aggregate of the features and traits that made up the nature of this man were not good. I was consistently unreliable, dishonest, and self-gratifying. There was no continuity in my life; my life looked different with my friends and buddies than it did with my wife and kids. I was a chameleon.

After the age of 32, following my conversion to Christianity, some real house cleaning took place. The good news about my story is that you *can* recover! You can take poor character and lack of integrity, your reputation, and you can turn them around. When I talk to people that have only known me over the past 15 years, they have a difficult time believing that I was the way I used to be; they are, in fact, astonished. Conversely, if one of my current friends within the last 15 years were to run into an old acquaintance or friend of mine from 25 years ago, and they were to begin talking about me, they would literally think they were talking about two different people – until they did a little fact checking with each other. It's pretty entertaining to run into people who haven't seen me in 20 years, those who knew the "old Allen." Then they see the new and improved Allen, and in the conversation they realize, I don't talk like I used to, I don't do the things I used to, and so on. There is this odd sort of surprised, confused, sometimes awkward interchange. I'm still "normal," but it's a new, better, normal compared to the life I led, and some of them till lead.

I teach my boys about the importance of the quality of their names and the way it is ultimately defined by their character and integrity, which in turn are defined by what they do and say on a consistent basis. They start with a clean slate. They tarnish it from time to time, and then we talk about how to clean it up and make it right.

I talk to my boys about the ability to recover, but that it takes a lot of work and effort to repair the quality of your name once you have tarnished it. That's why starting well, and living well, are so important. If you can instill this in your boys – the importance of the quality of their names – you have done well. This is an anchor for your journey with them. Next to faith, a man's character and integrity are the most important things he has, and the most enduring things he has. I've seen men of faith with a shortage of character or integrity, and it has been, or will be, the ruin of them. All their accomplishments will be forgotten if they fail here. Many a great man has been undone by a shortcoming in this area.

Personal Assessment – Spoke #1: Character & Integrity

1. Take an inventory of where you are personally.
   - Home Run – Why? What evidence is there?
   - Base Hit – Why? What evidence is there?
   - Strike Out – Why? What evidence is there?

2. What do you have to teach your son, either from doing it well or doing it wrong?
   - Where have you been successful, and what can you teach your son?
   - Where have you missed it, and what can you teach your son about it (what have you learned)?

3. What, if any, personal adjustments do you need to make to model well for your son?
   - As you assess your life currently against this spoke, Character and Integrity, what needs to change in order for there to be integrity with yourself and your son as you teach him to live well?

4. What resources do you need to equip your son in this area that either reinforce your success, or may augment where you may be lacking personally?
   - Search out resources and teaching tools: books, classes, videos, seminars, mentors, etc. that either help illustrate and support your strength here, or augment your weakness and create a strength in both you and your son.

Tip: Maybe for you, this is a simple process of looking at the areas of your life where you profess one thing, but your actions are inconsistent. Ask a few people close to you to give you some feedback. When you have identified a few areas of your character and integrity that need to be shored up, share them with your son, work on them, and allow him to hold you accountable as you work with him. Reading books together or watching documentaries, or observing people who model good character and integrity, will help both you and your son be inspired and motivated to aspire to greatness.

2nd SPOKE: DIRECTION
VALUES, VISION, GOALS

Children are not casual guests in our home. They have been loaned to us temporarily for the purpose of loving them and instilling a foundation of values on which their future lives will be built.

– James Dobson

The most pathetic person in the world is someone who has sight, but has no vision.

– Helen Keller

Goals are not only absolutely necessary to motivate us. They are essential to really keep us alive.

– Robert Schuller

THE TRIFECTA

This is an important spoke because of the significance of these three things in a person's life. Each one could possibly be a chapter in its own right. Entire books are dedicated to each area (values, vision, and goals). These three are closely linked to each other; they have a symbiotic relationship. In other words, they are dependent on each other, and you must possess them if you desire to live an intentional, purposeful life. You have values; whether or not you are consciously aware of them, whether or not they are stated, whether or not they are healthy, virtuous, and noble, you have them. You will follow a vision; either it will be someone else's, influenced by other forces or institutions or people, or it will be one specifically designed, thought out, and acted upon by you. You will have goals; they will either be random and by accident, determined and dictated by others, or intentionally designed by you.

Any one of these three if disconnected from the other two, is at one end of the spectrum incomplete, and at the other end, potentially dangerous. Values without vision or goals may make you a virtuous person, but you don't achieve or do anything significant in your life; it becomes mediocre and random. Vision without values is like a broken compass that doesn't give you the true north. If you start one degree off, it's no big deal for the first 100 feet. The farther you travel, however, the farther off course you become. You could end up anywhere, and most certainly not where you intended; it could put you in Bangor, Maine, when you had intended to end up in Bangor, Washington (3,000 miles apart from each other), on opposite sides of the continent. Goals without values or vision can produce "things" in your life, but your life may have no substance or purpose, and you end up empty, unfulfilled, and eventually wondering what life is even about.

I am not teaching about values, vision, and goals individually because this is not a book on goal setting. This is about making a boy into a man. These three things are not rocket science, although you can get into really interesting territory about them, especially as it relates to their power and influence regarding your mind and your life. My purpose is to create a compelling desire in your life to teach your boys to understand this important triad and see how the presence, or absence, of them will affect their lives.

ORDER TO AVOID CHAOS

Let's start with values. You have to have a core set of values to make sure that you are anchored to what matters most. It's much too easy to cast a vision and set goals and achieve them, only to find out you were off course. You get to the end, and you are either dissatisfied with the achievement, you have left a lot of damage in your wake, or you have become too self-absorbed.

Professionally, I have seen too many people climb the ladder of success only to find out it was leaning on the wrong wall. That's what I discovered when I finally achieved some level of financial success myself. At the end of the day, I had lost my marriage and my family. Now, if you would have asked me what I value most, I probably would have said, "Family," but it wasn't where I was spending my time and money. I certainly didn't have a vision, nor was I setting goals in alignment with that value. I have worked with a lot of people who have had the same experience. So one way to avoid the potential catastrophic consequences is to clarify your values. Know them, live them, apply them, let them be the filter for all your decisions, and you will live a much more fulfilling life. The basis for those values is of utmost importance. This would be your hub.

Vision comes next. A vision is just a broad picture of the different areas of your life, and what you want them to look like when you get to those stages in your life. Stephen Covey, in his book *Seven Habits of Highly Effective People,*[1] coined a phrase that many people use today: *Begin with the end in mind.* That's what we do with vision. You will help your boys identify things that are important to them individually, and develop a short-term vision for their future. It doesn't have to be for retirement, or 50 years from now, it can and should be shorter-term than that. In fact, at their age it should be much shorter than that. They can think about six months out, or maybe a year, or maybe through college, and from there they can develop their goals. Primarily, you want to help them create the habit of developing a vision, a tool they will use throughout their life. As they get older and more established, the vision can be longer, with an end-of-life perspective.

This leads to goals. Your goals should be in support of moving you toward your vision for your life, family, career, etc. Once you have a vision in place, you break the vision down into short-term goals, and with the achievement of those goals, the vision becomes a reality. The goals should be very short-term at this stage to correspond with young people's attention span. Above all, you want them to experience success with goal setting. Once they have this, you will have instilled in them the one effective habit that will put them head and shoulders above everyone else. Too many people are wandering around in life today, aimlessly. They don't have any goals that excite them, or that give them enthusiasm and motivation for the day. In the absence of exciting goals, life becomes drudgery, the obstacles become way too big, and people lose motivation. Lack of motivation is simply the absence of clear, compelling, and exciting goals.

There you have it: the sequence, and the "why." WARNING! Don't make the mistake I made with this process, rendering it way too complicated and intense. My personality is kind of like that, and

I made the process grueling at times. Don't do that to your boys. Keep it light, keep it simple, and let it be theirs. Resist the temptation to relive your youth through your boys and make up for all your mistakes; you will ruin the process…trust me on that one!

VALUES

I believe that values are most important because they are a statement of what matters most to you in life; they reflect your core set of beliefs and principles. I want to make sure that the vision and goals I set in my life are in alignment with my values, so I don't violate the things that are most important. Simply put, your values are the core things on which you place the most importance and you are unwilling to compromise. When I began this process with my first son, I wanted to hear certain values come from him. I learned after a while that at 13, he didn't have the same values as I did at 42. Go figure. So don't be disappointed; be encouraging. Guide them and help them understand the importance of values, but in the end, if the values are not theirs, they are useless and you've wasted your time.

I began by telling my sons what my values were and why I chose them. Again, I used the contrasts in my life to explain them, and as I mentioned earlier, how they were consistent with what God wants for me and my life. I had them brainstorm everything that was important to them, without judging the list as to whether I personally thought items were worthy as a value. I just wanted a brainstorming session. It took a little priming, but we got there. I saw things like golfing, playing video games, skateboarding, reading, playing with friends, swimming, and going on vacations. It took everything I had not to say, *"Are you kidding!"* What about family, faith, God, integrity, character, health, and so on? Okay, maybe I did say it out loud, but remember, learn from my mistakes!

My older son, Devan, began to reason with me a little bit; that's like him. I eventually realized the mistake I was making and backed off. It was a good thing I was learning this with my older son. My younger son is not so…tactful. By the time I got to him with his rite of passage, I was much more patient and open with the process. Our sons' values will change with time, just as ours did as we matured. Remember, it's more about the habit at this point. It is our habits, those habitual things we do, large and small, significant and seemingly insignificant, that will have a direct influence on the direction and quality of our lives. So helping them develop healthy habits is a critical part of being a father and raising your sons. I cannot make it a habit for them, I can only share the importance of it, and give them the opportunity to develop it. So the habit of writing down a vision will be very useful for them in helping with direction and decision-making in their lives.

What you are likely to see are a whole lot of little items that can be rolled up into one value. For example, with Brendan, my younger son, I saw things like riding my bike, riding my skateboard, and playing video games. As we talked about these things, I found the real value was spending time with his friends. Those were all activities *around* the value, and they could have been any number of things. So by asking him a few questions, we were able to identify the true value – friends – and, more specifically, having fun with friends.

You are also likely to see a long list of values when you are done with the brainstorming session, as in the case of my boys. Now, everything that I have read and understand about values is that fewer is better. You don't want a list of 20 values. Your son should be able to easily recite his values and remember they are the core things that matter, not *all* the activities. On the other hand, to become so dogmatic and only allow five, for example, is not good, either. Each son is different; my older son had five values, and my younger son had three. That's OK.

Once the values are identified and written down, we talk about what each value looks like in action. In other words, what does that value look like when you are living it? This is usually a paragraph or two, and/or bullets, that describe what they are doing, behaving, thinking, etc. that makes the value real. For example, one value may be having fun with friends. What does that look like? *"I am spending time regularly with friends doing a variety of activities, sometimes things I really like, other times things they like more than I. But we are doing something together."*

Another example of what a value might look like is something both boys put down as a value – family. For them, it sounded something like, *"I care about my family. I am respectful to everyone. I defend my family. I love my family, and we do things together a lot."* Simple enough, and whenever we get a little sideways, we can go back to their values, and the description of what it looks like, and we get right back on track. It's not me getting after them; it's them remembering what they wrote and what they value. Don't be discouraged by what they write down. After you've talked to them and they still put something down that seems a little goofy, roll with it. You have plenty of time with them to come back later and reassess their values…and you will.

Values Gap is a great exercise as you close the values activity with your sons, and on a recurring basis as a checkup. It's really very simple: have them state a value, and what they wrote out regarding what it looks like in action. Then have them consider the last 30 days, and ask them if their actions, decisions, and behaviors are consistent with their values. This is referred to as the "Values Gap."

If there is one, a gap that is between their declared values and their behaviors, talk to them about how they can close this gap.

VISION

With their values in place, I drew a little wheel with spokes in it (see diagram), creating six Vs. Each V represented an area of their life: recreational, vocational, educational, spiritual, health, and family. These could be any number of things, but these are what I determined to be the big six. I explained what each one was, and made it relevant to them. Recreation was playing, sports, outdoors, etc. Vocation was what they wanted to be when they grew up. Education was about school and college. Spiritual was about their spiritual growth as Christians. Health was about taking care of their bodies. And family was just that, family.

My goal was to have my sons formulate a single, defining statement that integrated the vision for each of these critical areas of their life. This would not be six different vision statements, but one statement, written in such a way that it naturally flowed and segued into each area, and talked about what will be. It is a grand, inclusive, and overarching statement, from a young boy's perspective, on what he wants his life, holistically, to look like.

I had them think about each area of their life one year out (approximately). I picked a significant date in the near future, and used that as the "point on the horizon" they were heading for, and what they would want that area of their life to look like from that point in time looking backwards, reflecting on the time gone by. It might have been the end of the school year when my son was 13, it might have been the end of high school as a junior, etc. It took a while, but it was fun. What it did was get them to think beyond the moment and realize that if they wanted something specific, it happens intentionally, not randomly. They had to determine, in advance, what kind of grades they wanted, how they wanted to grow as Christians, what they wanted to do for and with their family, what sports, if any, they wanted to participate in, and so on.

Remember to Keep It Super Simple (KISS) – learn from my mistakes. I was hoping to hear something like, *"I want to be an architect and graduate college a year early with honors, and build award-winning structures that are world renowned, and be a millionaire by the time I am 30."* What I got was *"I want good grades."* I was so disappointed and tried to conceal it, but I didn't do a very good job. I had to remember that they were only 13 or 14 years old. We worked on being a little more specific, and why that's important, but again I want to emphasize that this process belongs to them. If they don't own it, they won't care about it. We ended up with something like, *"I want a 3.5 GPA."* I had to help them understand that being vague or ambiguous doesn't help a person's mind find its way. Your mind needs a clear target to aim for, just as your eye needs a clear target when you are shooting target practice, or playing darts, pool, or other sports, for example.

It's truly amazing that the only chance you will have of intentionally hitting that target is when you are aiming at it and focusing on it intensely. A professional wide receiver will tell you he is focusing intently on the tip of the ball as it is coming toward him. You have to have a target for your mind. Imagine a nuclear missile being fired from a Trident Submarine without coordinates for a specific destination. You get the point.

We walked through this same process for each of the six Vs. I will tell you that I took these opportunities to talk to them about what they wanted 5, 10, and 20 years out, as well, but we didn't write them down. So the 3.5 GPA was in the context of going to college and having opportunities at scholarships. Going to college was in the context of wanting to be an architect or a business owner. It was fun talking with them, and getting them dreaming about what they could do and be. I never put any limits on their dreaming. I never said *"I don't know about that,"* or *"Are you sure you want to be that?"* I would ask them why they wanted to do or be something, and we would talk about the "why." Sometimes they would change their mind.

This is not complicated, but it takes some time. We spent a few weeks going over this process together. We'd have our Friday Starbucks time, talk about where they were in the process, and work on it over the next week. The following Friday, we'd make a little more progress. I will provide a rough outline of the time we spent in each area in Chapter 15, Developing Your Plan.

GOALS

Once we had a 12-month vision, we went to work on goals. The goals for each area were short-term ones that supported their vision, had supporting actions for each goal, and tangible benefits. The reason for all this goes back to the point I made in Vision about having a target for your mind. Your mind has a far greater likelihood of hitting the target the more specific and "do-able" the goal is, when you plan the steps for success, and, finally, when you give yourself a compelling reason for hitting the goal. There is a simple and effective process for writing goals for an area:

1. Write out the goal.
2. Identify the steps necessary to achieve the goal, and write them out.
3. Identify the compelling and tangible benefits of the goal, and write them out.
4. Review your goal regularly.

So for a 3.5 GPA, for example, it might look like this:

Goal: I maintain a B+ average in each of my six classes daily for 30 days (January 1-31), and I am so proud of myself.
Actions: I do my homework immediately after school, before I do anything that's fun. I am proactive in getting help from teachers if I don't understand my assignment. I turn in all my assignments on time daily and use class time well.
Benefits: I have the respect and praise of my parents and teachers. I enjoy the privileges of maintaining my grades, like driving my car. I increase my chances for scholarships and grants for college. I have personal pride in my achievement. I have my $20 bill from my parents for the month.
3x5 Cards: Put this information on a 3x5 card. Put the goal on the front, and the actions and benefits on the back. The purpose of the card is to be handy for your sons and readily accessible, removing excuses and inconvenience.

Review and visualize: *The most important step* – This entire activity runs the risk of being nothing more than a waste of your son's time, and yours, if you don't do this last step. It is IMPERATIVE that your sons review their 3x5 cards at least twice a day, once in the morning when they are relaxed, before they get going, and again in the evening, maybe just before bed, before they are too tired.

Goal: I maintain a B+ average in each of my six classes daily for 30 days (January 31) and I am so proud of myself.

Actions: I do my homework immediately after school before I do anything fun. I am proactive in getting help from teachers if I don't understand my assignment; I turn in all my assignments on time daily and use class time well.

Benefits: I have the respect and praise of my parents and teachers; I enjoy the privileges of maintaining my grades like driving my car; I increase my chances for scholarships and grants for college; I have personal pride in my achievement; I have my $20 bill from my parents for the month.

When they review the cards, they just need to take a moment to see themselves "as if" they had achieved the goal. This could be simply seeing themselves holding their report card showing all B+s or the 3.5 GPA, or driving down the road in the car, smiling at themselves in the rear view mirror, or receiving that $20 bill in their hand. It only takes about 30 seconds per goal for this whole process. It is not time consuming. It is not helpful to read the cards as they are running out the door, or falling asleep in the middle of the statements. If you can convince and motivate them to do it more frequently, all the better. This is the PRIMARY reason people don't achieve their goals. They take the time to go through some goal-setting activity (good or bad), and then they just become wishes, hopeful thinking, or resolutions because they fail to review and visualize their goals.

Use your mind as a tool. The goal, the steps, and the benefits are all stated personally *(I)*, positively *(proud, proactive, respect, privileges, pride, $20,)* and present tense *(maintain, do, am, have, enjoy, increase)*. This is particularly important. Without getting into the psychology of the steps, this would become a different book altogether, suffice it to say that your mind has a much higher likelihood of helping you achieve goals when it thinks of your goals, actions, and benefits in the "now." When that is accompanied by reviewing and visualizing, with emotion attached and motivation assigned as described above, look out; your mind becomes a heat-seeking missile searching for its target!

This entire process outlined above for writing goals only takes a few minutes for each goal, and it's simple. Your boys can see 30 days ahead; they have a much harder time staying focused on 12 months out. When they see the simple activities they need to focus on to hit their goal, it feels do-able to them. And when they know what's in it for them, they are more motivated. If they stay on the 30-day goals, the vision will take care of itself! You will be sitting down with them about every 30 days to identify the next 30-day goals. If you and your son set a goal for each area of their life (the "V" diagram in vision), then at most they have six goals. However, that may be too much for your son. If that is the case, then prioritize the areas of vision, and the goals. Don't overwhelm your son. Remember the goal of this activity is to help him develop a successful habit that will serve him throughout his life and set him apart as the top 5% of the people in the world who are intentional and focused. So whatever you do, don't let him feel discouraged and defeated; work with him and his capacity, and help him experience success with his goals.

REINFORCEMENT

There are a million teaching moments throughout this process. Don't miss a single one! For example, when we were talking about grades, I would use that time to talk about education, college, career, and financial success. I would then take some time with them and drive around different parts of our community, both affluent ones and less affluent. I would ask them in which community they would prefer to raise their family. I would show them grown men working minimum wage jobs, and then show them men working at much higher wages with skills, or owning a business, and ask them which they would prefer. Note that I was very careful not to judge people. I explained that some people end up in circumstances and situations, not because of their own doing, but because life throws curve balls. I was also very careful to make sure that they knew the people who weren't as well off were not less worthy or important or valuable. The purpose was to show them the importance of their choices and decisions.

Remember the Bible? In the book of Proverbs, over and over again, it emphasizes hard work, being self-disciplined, etc. It says in one verse, *"A little sleep, a little slumber, a little folding of the hands and poverty will creep up on you"* (Proverbs 6:9-11 and 24:32-34). I would help them to understand that a lot of those people had the life they did because of their choices, such as laziness or lack of self-discipline with finances, or wrong attitudes about work, or thinking that someone owed them something. My boys know they are to never look down on another human being. We are to have empathy and care for everyone. But not everyone is the same, and no one is exempt from the law of sowing and reaping; as a man sows, so shall he reap.

PATIENCE – CHINESE BAMBOO TREE

So that is direction: values, vision, and goals. When you are done, your son should have his values clarified and know what they look like in action. He should have a vision that incorporates each of the six areas for his life for the next 12 months. He should have 30-day goals, one for each area of his life. I am not going to deceive you: this takes discipline and time on your part. It will be easy, at times, to put it off because they won't remember, or other things will be competing for your time. But this isn't about today. This is about 10 years from now, and the habits and disciplines you want your boys to have. It's about your vision for your family 20, 30, or 40 years from now. Stay with it, Dad. Your sons are like the Chinese Bamboo tree. You plant it, feed it, and water it. For four years you see nothing, no growth whatsoever. You will wonder, "Is anything happening"? Then in the fifth, year that bamboo tree explodes and grows by as much as 90 feet during the growing season, which is only about six weeks. All this is predicated on the right growth environment. You may not see the growth externally, at first, with your boys, but trust the process and create the right growth environment; roots are growing deep within your son that will make him strong and enable explosive growth in the future.

PERSONAL ASSESSMENT – SPOKE #2: DIRECTION

1. Take an inventory of where you are personally.
    *   Home Run – Why? What evidence is there?
    *   Base Hit – Why? What evidence is there?
    *   Strike Out – Why? What evidence is there?

2. What do you have to teach your son, either from doing it well or doing it wrong?
    *   Where have you been successful, and what can you teach your son?
    *   Where have you missed it, and what can you teach your son about it (what have you learned)?

3. What, if any, personal adjustments do you need to make to model well for your son?
    *   As you assess your life currently against this spoke, Direction, what needs to change in your life in order for there to be integrity with yourself and your son as you teach him to live well?

4. What resources do you need to equip your son in this area that either reinforce your success, or may augment where you may be lacking personally?
    *   Search out resources and teaching tools: books, classes, videos, seminars, mentors, etc. that either help illustrate and support your strength here, or augment your weakness and create a strength in both you and your son.

Tip: Begin by looking at your own values, and look for gaps in what you profess and what you do, and where you spend your time and money. If you say family is your highest value, is this where you are spending your greatest amount of financial and time resources? Do you have a vision for your own life 12, 24 or 36 months from now, let alone 25 years from now? Do you set goals for yourself and review them, and aspire and work toward them? If you have not had much teaching or experience in values clarification, vision development, and goal setting, sit down with someone who has, get his input, and ask for his guidance. Simply apply what you have learned here. There is no shortage of books, seminars, and teachings on these subjects. So do some research, ask someone whom you respect what books, CD's, etc. he would recommend for you and your son. This is not as daunting as it may seem.

3rd SPOKE: CHIVALRY
HOW TO TREAT A WOMAN

Some say that the age of chivalry is past, that the spirit of romance is dead. The age of chivalry is never past, so long as there is a wrong left unredressed on earth.

– Charles Kingsley

THE PERFECT STORM

This was one of the catalysts for writing this book: In many ways, women have become nothing more than objects for men, and our culture has reduced them to nothing more than common "eye candy."

Just look at billboards, television advertisements, and football games. How about the latest rage - bikini baristas at coffee shops? I will drive down the road, sometimes, in my town and see young girls walking down the street, and I cannot believe how they are dressed. I think to myself (and sometimes out loud), *"What father just lets his daughter walk out of the house like that"?* Don't get me wrong; I'm not a prude. I still have some testosterone left in my body, and I was a teenager at one time. I remember what it was like to begin noticing girls and my hormones being stirred up. And that is exactly why I am concerned today. For you men who grew up in the '70s and '80s as I did, you would probably agree that girls and women today are less modest and discreet, and our culture is much more sexualized and unrestrained as compared to then. The combination is not good.

Just do a little research on sexual activity taking place today in schools, and you will be stopped in your tracks. In a study in 2009 by the CDC[1], Youth Risk Behavior Surveillance – United States 2009, conducted among students in grades 9-12, the following information is recorded nationwide: 46% of students had already had sexual intercourse, 34.2% were currently sexually active, 5.9% had sexual intercourse before age 13, 13.8% have had sex with four or more persons (I can't imagine what the number is for 2 or more), and 34.2% had had sexual intercourse with at least one person in the last 3 months. There is a lot more information in that study that correlates drug use to teen sex, use of protective measures, and so on. This was 2009, so there is a very strong possibility that these numbers have gotten worse as our culture and media have only gotten more flagrant about discarding traditional values and virtue.

There is something very important to remember: these statistics are for "sexual intercourse," and thanks to former President Bill Clinton, we all know what kind of sexual activity is not classified as sexual intercourse. Why do I bring that up? Because if you included oral sex in that study, the numbers would literally shock you! It's not that kids were not sexually promiscuous in the 70's and 80's, they were, but the level and type of that activity is exponentially worse. And more importantly, the type of activity and the degrading nature of it toward girls are alarming, demonstrating a complete lack of respect for them on the part of boys. I read a book a few years ago called *Battle Cry for a Generation*, by Ron Luce.[1] *Battle Cry* reported on the sexual activity that is going on inside the schools, not just sexual intercourse, but other sexual acts, as well. My heart breaks as I write this, but young women are performing oral sex on boys at school regularly. Does it get any more degrading than that? The reason I have included this information in this chapter, rather than Sexual Integrity (next chapter), is because this chapter is about men protecting women, honoring and respecting them, rather than exploiting them.

I am not putting every girl and every boy into these categories, but you may be surprised, at least I was, with the initial revelation of this information. It's rampant, it's dehumanizing, it's devaluing, and it's happening in your schools during school hours. It has become acceptable for girls and women to dress in ways that draw specific attention to all the sexual parts of their bodies. It can be difficult enough for a grown man with character and self-control driving down the street, walking in the mall, working in an office, or even sitting in church not to be challenged, let alone for the young teenage boy.

HOW LOW CAN WE GO?

What about a young man who hasn't fully developed these qualities of character and self-discipline? And to make a finer point, many men have not developed the self-control and character in their own lives, and have not instilled it in their sons. You cannot give your son what you don't have, but you will give him what you do have. This isn't about sex, but this is the foundational problem, I believe, that leads to attitudes toward women on the part of men, that produces all the ancillary behaviors that result in women not being honored and respected and treated appropriately. We have lost our way as men. There was a day when the word "chivalry" meant something, when a man would honor and protect a woman's virtue and femininity.

Not long ago, but what seems to have been in a land far, far away, if a man saw a woman being treated poorly, he would not stand by idly and pretend it was not happening. It brings back to my mind a movie called *Back to the Future.* In the movie, George McFly, a little guy, is faced with a difficult situation: a girl, Lorraine, is in the back seat of a car being attacked by a physically imposing guy and bully named Biff. George has a choice to make; either he defends Lorraine at significant personal risk, or he turns and walks away and leaves her to Biff. He chooses to protect her. It was a great choice, the right choice.

Courage will be required and risk will be involved with chivalry. There was something noble and virtuous about protecting a woman's honor, even if she was a stranger. In 2009, there was a 15-year-old girl who was brutally sexually abused by multiple boys while another crowd of boys stood around and watched.[3] This happened in school! This is not isolated. I don't know where you live in the United States, but no doubt you have the same horrific stories happening in your community. They are happening with alarming frequency. Just follow the news for a couple of weeks and you'll have all the evidence you need that we have sunk to new lows in our society.

The question remains, though, how low can we go?

Where are the men? Where are the real men-in-training? Where was the boy in the group whose father trained him up to respect and protect a woman, who in that moment had the courage and outrage, righteous anger, if you will, to step up and say, "Enough," and maybe even put himself in harm's way for what is right; she is someone's sister and daughter. I don't care about the details of how she got into that situation, but what happened was just a thermometer that took the cultural temperature, and it was a new low. Just for the record, my boys know that if they, are in a situation like that, they have only one choice, get involved; be a George McFly.

THE PROBLEM IS THE SOLUTION

So how did we get here? Great question. In both cases (girls and boys), it's the failure of the dads. In the case of young girls and adult women who don't have enough self-respect, value, and esteem, it's a dad's failure. In the case of young boys and adult men who don't have the character, self-discipline, and honor to hold women in esteem, it's a dad's failure. I wish I could say that's not the case, but I know it's true. We can look at lots of data from sociologists, psychologists, etc., but it doesn't really take all that to know what the problem is. It's obvious to anyone who wants to look.

It is widely known now that young girls who behave inappropriately often suffer from a lack of strong self-worth, acceptance, and unconditional love, and they are missing the protective covering of the confident, appropriate, and strong love of a father. Who a woman is today, and how she behaves, is largely influenced and shaped by her self-perception, based on the security she had in her father's love. The more secure a girl is in her father's healthy love, and the more appropriate attention she gets from her father, the less attention-seeking behavior she will exhibit. Nurtured in this kind of atmosphere, you would see more confident young girls and women who do not seek the validation that they are beautiful and valuable from boys and young men, who can't see beyond the filter of raging hormones.

I have to stop here on this subject – that of a father and his daughter – because this is about a father and his sons. I think this is so important because, if we can raise boys well, they will be good fathers. If we have good fathers, we'll have far fewer issues with vulnerable and lost girls. I believe that we fathers are the root cause and the primary solution.

It's entirely possible that you just simply don't care about all this, although I doubt it. I think you would have closed this book a couple of chapters ago. If you have read this far, you have taken some personal responsibility and know deep in your heart that YOU ARE THE SOLUTION! We need to get our heads in the game with our boys, because whether you realize it or not, you already have skin in the game, so you have a vested interest to begin raising boys who have a strong moral compass, courage, and character, who above all things honor the tenderness, softness, and vulnerability of a woman.

UNINTENDED CONSEQUENCES

The women's movement, and more specifically feminism, over the last several decades has done significant damage to women and our society. Women got, in large part, what they wanted; they just had no idea of what they were asking for. This issue is extensively and well articulated in the book *The Flipside of Feminism*, by Phyllis Schlafly and Suzanne Venker.[4] In the feminists' quest for equality, they have strived to make women equal but they are not.

The Bible calls them the weaker vessel. It is not a derogatory statement; it is simply a truth that any logical, right-minded person, male or female, understands. It doesn't have anything to do with standing, worth, intellect, capabilities, and the like. It has strictly to do with the fact that women were designed to come under the covering and protection of men. The reference refers, in part, to the fact that women were created with different physical attributes, they are smaller are less muscular (with a few exceptions), and need someone stronger, physically, to protect them and watch over them. A young girl or woman properly loved and cared for can grow, flourish, and achieve under the covering of a good husband or father. I realize this is an abhorrent statement for a feminist to read, but it is true. To be sure, a woman can grow, flourish, and achieve without a good father or husband, but there is a part of her, an authentic femininity and tenderness, that is either never developed or is underdeveloped by being outside the care of an authentic, good man. She can be free and safe to discover and express herself fully as a woman, and her personhood is fully intact and not diminished in any way. I said the *covering* and *protection* of men, not the abuse by them: Not verbal, not emotional, not physical. They are not "less than" men; they are meant, nearly above all other things, to be cherished.

What has been the unintended consequence of the women's movement, which I believe is also part of a larger movement away from moral and social standards established by God? Many men simply don't care. Men have lost a large part of their purpose as men. Their role as protector has been taken away, and rather than fight for it, men have acquiesced and relegated the role, or neglected

131

it altogether. How long does a man need to be told he's not needed before he simply no longer cares? How long does a woman need to be told she doesn't need a man before she ultimately believes, *"I don't need a man."* How many times does a man need to be portrayed as a hapless idiot on television and in movies before it begins to be reflected in our own attitudes and culture? The result has been that we have fallen out of the rightful order of things, and chaos has resulted. We have allowed a lie to replace the transcendent truth most people innately understand.

In all fairness to women, there was decay in how boys were being trained up, as well, and there was a gap that was emerging. Could a woman really trust that a man would properly care for her, cover and protect her, and allow her to be fully free, to be who she was created to be? If there wasn't a question mark in the minds of women as to whether they could trust men, then maybe the whole women's liberation movement might not have gotten traction. I am not throwing the baby out with the bath water, either. There was much that needed to be addressed in regards to women's equal standing, but it was not nearly the issue it was made up to be. Feminism is less about redressing wrongs; it's more about advancing ideology and fundamentally changing our culture, and rejecting the designed order ordained by God.

Where has feminism taken us? A word of warning: this story is a bit graphic, but completely telling. I recently watched a television news magazine show, and it told the story of how women, in some cases, who wanted children, but didn't want the "baggage" of a man, were finding men online and meeting them in hotels to buy their sperm. The man would go into the bathroom, masturbate, and then give the woman his sperm. She would immediately inject it into her uterus with a plastic syringe, and then either stay in the hotel for a few hours with her hips elevated, or be driven home in the back seat of the car with her hips elevated, in the hopes of getting pregnant. In one of the stories, the woman who bought the donor sperm was driven home by her female partner. This is where, in part, feminism has taken us.

THE GOOD FIGHT

Men, we can change the course of this trend if we will take back our responsibility, back up, and train our boys on how to be real men. Let's not just give up on our boys and, consequently, our society; let's fight the good fight! You may even feel defeated yourself as a man, but we were not designed to sit around and lick our wounds, full of self-pity. If our strength fails, we are lost for sure. We can train up a new generation of boys that will return to the character-led values that put women back in the place of honor and esteem, and women will respond.

Does this sound ridiculous to you? It's not. All you have to do is spend a day with my boys and me. Watch how women respond when my boys open a door for them. Watch the reaction when they see them pull out a chair for a woman. Watch the response when they order the menu item at the restaurant for her. Here's the deal though. You will notice a startled and pleasant response from slightly older women; I'd say, mid-thirties and above. What you will see in younger women and girls is a weird look, as if to say, *"What are you doing?"* And that is the point of the matter. They don't expect it, and it is strange to them; they don't even know how to respond to common courtesy and honor because they don't experience it. My daughter gets that treatment now, and has for years, from my boys and myself. My boys just know to do this for their sister, mother, grandmother, or any woman for that matter. It is the norm in our house. Two things are resulting. My daughter isn't going to put up with some numbskull that doesn't have the good sense to treat her as she deserves, and my boys aren't going to be with a girl long who doesn't respond to his excellent behavior.

If we, as men, would raise our boys to be the kind of men that highly regard women, respect them, treat them as worthy of such kind regard and respect, they would respond. Seriously, what woman does not want a man who cares for her, protects her, opens the door for her, pulls out the chair for her, orders her food for her, cherishes her, and believes she is worthy of personal sacrifice? What woman would not walk more confidently and securely? But that is not the reality for many girls today, and, consequently, for women as they grow up. What would happen if the young girl who is seeking validation and love gives herself over to some hormone-drenched young man, and he says, *"No, you are far too important and valuable"?*

IT'S AN ATTITUDE THING

I said earlier in this chapter that we fathers are the solution. It begins with raising boys with proper attitudes toward women, raising them counter-culture, to cherish women as a gift, and to protect and honor a woman, rather than expose and exploit her. We could talk about the symptoms all day long and not solve the problem, because we are not dealing with the root. If a plant is sick, check the root system. If our culture is sick, check the root system – dads. Boys raised properly become dads. Dads with the right values and attitudes toward women raise different kinds of girls and boys, and we begin to make a difference. We must begin with the root, and let the tree become healthy as it grows.

What specifically am I talking about here when I talk about proper attitudes and values? How many of you know guys with pin-ups in their garages? How many of you know guys that are drooling over the cheerleaders on the Sunday NFL game? How many of you know guys who are glued to the TV during the Victoria's Secret commercials? How many of you know guys with their porn magazines or Internet sites? How many of you know men who don't open doors for their wives or daughters? How many of you know guys who tell sex jokes about women? How many of you know men who stare at women walking down the street, or in the mall, or at work? This is just a short list of disrespectful behaviors. You might even be one of those guys. Many guys don't even understand the consequences of their behavior on their sons and daughters. They were raised by dads who didn't get it, either. I was. Why the emphasis on sex and sexualizing our sons in a chapter on chivalry? Simple, because it is at the core of what develops the attitudes in our sons, that produces the behaviors that devalue and objectify women. Our behaviors are our beliefs acted upon.

Many of our dads were raised in a culture with slowly eroding core values. The values that used to influence proper male behavior began to be redefined, and we lost the sense of our ideal identity as men. This didn't happen overnight, and it won't change overnight, but just as sure as it did change, it can change back. Progress is all well and fine, and many good things come from progress, but some things were not meant to be progressive, and values are one of those things.

So what about the guy described above? What message is he sending to his sons and daughters about the value of women? To his daughter…you are an object, and by being like those women you get the attention of men you admire, chiefly your dad. To his son…this is what men do and this is what women are, objects to lust over and fantasize about, the exact opposite of respect and honor. Is it any wonder we have the problems we have today? Not every man is like that guy; he may be more passive or discreet about it, he may casually participate in it, he may not make a stand against it with his buddies...and his boy is watching. What is his boy learning? He is learning a lack of moral courage. When these attitudes are formed early on, they stick, and they are extremely difficult to change. It's hard enough with your boys being at school, associating with guys whose dads don't care, in a culture that doesn't care. What chance do they have now living in a home where the dad doesn't care, either? What chance do young girls have in this predicament?

BE THE SOLUTION

This means at times, men, we have to fight our own tendencies, but isn't that what maturity is all about? We do what we have to do, rather than what we want to do; that's what being a man is all about. We do what is best for others, rather than what is best for us. I know that each man will have a different struggle in this area. Some guys won't struggle with "looking" (or lusting) at other women. Some guys will have an enormous struggle with it. Some guys won't have any problem with porn, and other guys will have an enormous struggle with it. There are tools and help for every man who wants it, but you have to want it, and if raising a son who knows how to authentically treat a woman properly isn't enough...then what is? You may have a daughter. What kind of boy do you want your next door neighbor to be raising: the horn dog boy who is obsessed with sex and whose only attitude toward women is a demeaning one, or do you hope that his dad is raising a son who honors, respects, and reveres women as co-created equals to be cherished?

You're that man next door! Be the solution. Look around you for a moment, and ask yourself this simple question: Culturally, are we better today, or are we worse? What kind of boy are you going to raise, and what kind of man will he be? You will decide, to be sure. By doing something, you will decide, or by doing nothing, you will decide.

This spoke is less about simply going through a book, and more about the ongoing behaviors and dialogue my sons and I have. We talk at length about what they see in our home versus what they see elsewhere. We observe constantly those around us in public places, at dinners, or with family, observing all the things men are, or are not, doing. I am constantly pointing out things around us that demean or marginalize women, and they get it. We spend a lot of time in the Bible on this subject, because it has much to say about the attitudes a man should have toward a woman. Of course, I do my best to set a great example for my boys, and they see the benefit as my lovely wife reciprocates. They have also seen times when I haven't done such a stellar job, and how my wife responds. My boys get to see how a woman properly loved and cared for responds.

My boys also realize that a woman who doesn't respond to his proper and respectful behavior may not be a woman that he needs to be investing time with. She will not respect him or his values, and that usually means she has conflicting values. As I close this chapter, it is important to understand that we, as adult men, have to take responsibility for our environment. We may have not personally created the problem, but are we perpetuating it? Have we been immersed in this coarse culture so long that we have a generation that doesn't realize it hasn't always been this way, one that thinks this is normal? Chivalry is a man protecting a woman's honor rather than exploiting her. It's not a dead virtue if it lives in you, dad.

Personal Assessment – Spoke #3: Chivalry

1. Take an inventory of where you are personally.
   - Home Run – Why? What evidence is there?
   - Base Hit – Why? What evidence is there?
   - Strike Out – Why? What evidence is there?

2. What do you have to teach your son, either from doing it well or doing it wrong?
   - Where have you been successful, and what can you teach your son?
   - Where have you missed it, and what can you teach your son about it (what have you learned)?

3. What, if any, personal adjustments do you need to make to model well for your son?
   - As you assess your life currently against this spoke, Chivalry, what needs to change in your life in order for there to be integrity with yourself and your son as you teach him to live well in this spoke?

4. What resources do you need to equip your son in this area that either reinforce your success, or may augment where you may be lacking personally?
   - Search out resources and teaching tools: books, classes, videos, seminars, mentors, etc. that either help illustrate and support your strength here, or augment your weakness and create a strength in both you and your son.

Tip: This may be a great area to step up your game. You may not have thought much about the simple things in regard to how to treat a woman, let alone the bigger issues. Begin now; what aren't you doing that you can begin doing that your son can observe? And beyond that, he can do these things himself for his mother, sister, and other women. Ask your wife, if you have one, how she would like to be treated. She may not even know how to respond, or she may simply say you're "fine." I have taught my boys that fine means failure. This may be awkward for both you and your wife, but press on and insist that, if she could be treated how she dreamed, what would it look like? Keep in mind, your wife may have never been treated with the kind of respect, dignity, and honor she deserves by the men in her life, so this may be uncomfortable for her, as well. Begin to do those things, even if she resists at first, start with the small things, and move up. Be consistent.

4th SPOKE: SEXUAL INTEGRITY
NO DO OVERS

Run from sexual sin! No other sin so clearly affects the body as this one does. For sexual immorality is a sin against your own body.

– The Apostle Paul

WHAT'S IN A WORD?

Today, we hear a lot of the same messages, just redefined and repackaged, to get us to listen again to what we probably should already know and use. Sexual integrity is no different. Sexual purity is a great goal and a great term. But I like the word integrity.

Definition of *integrity* (according to Webster):

> 1. Firm adherence to a code, especially moral values – incorruptibility

> 2. An unimpaired condition - soundness

> 3. The quality or state of being complete or undivided – completeness

How's that for defining your sexuality? Uncorrupted, sound, an unimpaired condition, being complete and undivided. So sexual integrity could be stated this way:

Sexually uncorrupted, sound, uncompromised, unimpaired, and complete.

FAILURE IS NOT FINAL

I know full well this subject might be the one we fold on the quickest. We live in a culture that is so hyper-sexualized that it feels like one of those waves you get caught in while body surfing in Maui: it picks you up, slams you down, and then the current keeps you under and throws you around until you don't know which way is up. But just because it's hard, doesn't mean that it's not worthy of all our passionate effort to raise the bar. We should set an expectation and hold it high, then coach, encourage, and train our sons in how to maintain sexual integrity. The reality is that, by this definition, you may even be challenged yourself with your behavior in this area. That's okay. Raise your personal expectations, but don't lower the bar for your son simply because you're not there yet.

If you feel any shame in maybe having missed the mark yourself as a young man, don't! Shame will be a weapon used against you to make you feel you don't have the right, the credibility, or the knowledge to raise your boy differently. But you do! Thomas Edison learned to make the light bulb by making a lot of mistakes. He learned from them, and then got it right. How about you? Which attitude are you going to take? I would suggest you have a unique vantage point; you may know the damage, hurt, pain, dysfunction, and other very real consequences of sexual promiscuity personally and directly. Furthermore, if you're a Christian, shame has been dealt with. Where it may be an effective tool in the moment to correct behavior, shame is an insidious weapon used against you long-term to make you ineffective. God knew shame would be one of the primary issues that would keep you on the sidelines, rather than on the field advancing. That's why he put it to death on the cross with his Son. No one can remove your feelings of shame; you have to let them go yourself. Let it go. You cannot afford to let your son(s) wander off and lose his own way while you wallow in self-pity and shame, and not be there to lead him.

A person very close to me recently told me that I was naïve to believe my kids could have sexual integrity and remain virgins until marriage. I know the attitudes about this subject – and that is all the more reason to push back. Knowing what I know about how people think and how our minds work, I believe this comment came from the person's own failing as a parent. They wanted to believe that I was naïve and foolish, to avoid taking personal responsibility for their *own* failure. They needed to rationalize this to feel better about themselves and justify their shortcomings. We all do this to varying degrees and in different areas of our lives. What that person doesn't know is that I have lots of examples of people in my life today that raised their kids well and have experienced the blessings of sexual integrity.

TWO SIDES OF THE SAME COIN

This is one of those areas that is too vague and difficult to talk about without bringing our worldview into the conversation. This is because there are two fundamental views about our bodies and our sexuality:

View One – The popular cultural context: Sex is for my personal gratification, a physical act only. My body is mine. I can do what I want; no harm, no foul; everyone is doing it; I'm not responsible for, or to, anyone else; there's no accountability; I'll just be safe. This view also sees sex as THE expression of love.

View Two – The biblical context: Sex is the ultimate encounter intended to be shared with only one other person, a physical act with strong ramifications for your mind and soul and spirit. My body is not mine. I'm free to do what I want, but there are serious and long-term consequences. I am accountable to my future mate, her parents, my parents, and to God. This view sees sex as AN expression of love, a part, that when taken from the whole, is empty.

HEADS – THE POPULAR CULTURAL CONTEXT

View One is the easy one and the easy way. It's been an openly accepted part of our culture since the '60s. "Make love and not war" was the mantra. This was the prevailing attitude, and some of us still believe it today. It's that attitude that has created a worldwide epidemic of fatherless children, teen pregnancies, HIV/AIDS, emotionally destroyed people, dysfunctional lives, ruined marriages, and devastated families. And homosexuality is no different, just a different target for the passions. We like to live in some alternative reality where we think our actions have no consequences. In reality, there are consequences for every decision. And sex is one of the most dangerous areas about which to relax, because it is such a powerful force.

Sex is one of the strongest forces used to exploit our weakness and derail our lives as men. It offers no equivalent in immediate, powerful gratification. We are driven by a fundamental, powerful drive to mate, while simultaneously leaving us deeply unfulfilled just through the sexual experience alone. What do you get when you combine these things: powerful drive, instant gratification, unfulfilled experiences, all in the midst of a morally bankrupt culture? You have the potential for one messy, out of control situation. Take our primal desire devoid of any boundaries or accountability, a culture that winks and nods approval, and a severely damaged value structure, and we have a complete loss of sexual integrity. It's evidenced by the way we have normalized the lifestyle of the likes of Hugh Heffner, the founder and creator of *Playboy* magazine, and the subsequent explosion of the porn industry, promiscuous lifestyles, and the continuing degraded culture it propagated. We make sex outside of marriage look romantic and loving on our television shows and in movies, and portray it as if it's the norm. And the age in which these activities are being normalized on television and in movies is getting younger and younger.

Hey, when I was younger, I could not have cared less about this stuff that I am writing about now. It was all about me satisfying my appetite. I could not have cared less about anyone else, certainly not the object of my attention and desire. It was a clear message from home. It's a part of growing up, everyone does it; just be smart, and at least try to be safe. Ironically, it is viewed by many a dad, boy, and man as part of a boy's rite of passage. What a perversion of the very idea of a rite of passage!

Then there is love. We fall in love, or at least think we fall in love, and we want to be close and intimate with that special woman, so we do, because our society has, for the most part, been duped into believing the great deception. We have come to believe that sex is the ultimate expression of love. First thing, it's usually "lust" not love. Our emotions have deceived us into thinking we are in love. Second, our culture has deceived us into thinking that if we have sex, we have done the only natural thing between two people in love. This is a partial truth. First, every one of us has been what we thought was "in love," only to find out that it wasn't love at all. It was puppy love, or it was our eyes full of a beauty and a body that fooled us into thinking we were in love, or it was infatuation with an image or an idea. Second, in reality, the truest form of love is expressed in self-sacrifice, and in honoring and protecting a woman's most precious God-given gift, her virginity, until you know she is the one, and you have married her first. Anything less is NOT love, it is selfish gratification.

The other truth is that we just wanted to have sex. We were young, virile, hyper-stimulated, hounded by peer pressure (mostly lying boys and men), and we weren't taught any self-control, traditional values, and certainly not talked to about sexual integrity. I wasn't taught these things, so I don't expect many of you were, either. Today, our boys are told that abstinence is stupid and unrealistic, so make sure you have a condom just in case you don't have self-control. On top of that, girls aren't taught anything different, and they have been conditioned to become much more aggressive than they have ever been. In addition, girls are told it's just fine to wear next to nothing, and what they do have on is as tight as a second skin.

TAILS – THE BIBLICAL CONTEXT

View Two of sexual integrity begins on a very similar path: the power and the attraction are real. The natural hard wiring to mate is no less at play. The difference is that I actually have an education and understanding of what sex really is, and what its purpose is. The problem is, in part, an education issue. I don't mean education as the culture sees it, as Planned Parenthood sees it, or as the public schools see it. I mean a far deeper and transcendent awareness and education. This is where there is a clear line drawn in regards to your attitude about sex. When I became a Christian and began to read and understand how God had created us, and how he intended things to operate, I was completely blown away! There is no third option concerning attitudes about sexuality; it's either a view devoid of a creator, and devoid of a belief in a God with a plan and purpose, or a view *with* God as the principal architect and planner. Our culture is directly at odds with the Bible and God's expressed design…both views cannot be right.

View One is about sexual "liberation," subject to each individual's beliefs about sex. View Two is about sexual integrity, subject to God's clearly articulated truths about sex. There is a difference between personal belief and truth. There is truth. Not many want to hear that or believe that…I sure didn't. But let's just keep this in the context of the subject – sex. If each of us thinks our personal attitude (belief) about sex is right, then we could potentially have billions of "truths," one for each person on the planet. We don't have to agree on everything, but we can agree that this would be ridiculous to any educated person. The mathematical equation 2+2 = 4, that is true. The law of gravity is true, even if we may not agree on it. There are many things that influence our lives that are actual truths. It's when we get into personal moral issues that we generally decide there is no longer a truth, because we don't want to be denied our pleasure.

THE POWER OF SEX

Do you realize what actually happens when you have sex? You might, as I describe some things to you. But I want you to put the pieces together, so that you can make a really good and wise decision about what you believe. This will determine what you do with your boys, and it will ultimately shape their beliefs. I said in View One that sex is a physical act, and View Two states it's a physical act that affects your mind, your soul, and your spirit. It's physical, just as it is in View One, but it's so much more than that. It's *mind* because of what happens in your brain, and it's *soul* because of what happens with your attachments, and it's *spirit*, because of the issue that your body is not your own.

Psychologically, sex burns images into a person's subconscious mind that will never go away. Any man that has had more than one sexual partner knows this is true. You will have images in your brain forever. And because of the way our brains work, those memories can be recalled at any time. This is because the chemicals released during sex burn these experiences into your brain. You may say, "So what?" when you're young, but it's kind of like tattoos – when you get older and you can't get rid of them, you often wish you had never gotten them. These mental tapes will run randomly, and you can't get rid of them. And when you have settled down in your life with your wife, you will have regrets.

We are creatures that are more than just our physical bodies.

Our souls are the seat of our emotions. You may have heard the expression "soul ties" before. When we have sex, it extends beyond the physical attachment and literally creates a soul tie. We leave a little part of ourselves with each person, and we pick up a little part of each person with whom we have sex. That soul tie stays forever, and it's a powerful attachment. When the time comes that we find the person we will, ideally, be with for the rest of our lives, we don't have our whole sexual being to present to them, and we bring only a part, rather than the whole, because we have left parts of ourselves with others. Not only that, when you finally find your wife, or your son finds his wife, he brings all those other partners into the sexual relationship with his wife. And if she, too, has lacked sexual integrity, she brings the same issues to the relationship. Do you really want to bring all that baggage to your one true love?

Finally, spiritually, if you are a Christian, or become a Christian, the Apostle Paul tells us in 1 Corinthians, chapter 6, verses 15 through 18: *"Don't you realize that your bodies are actually parts of Christ? Should a man take his body, which is part of Christ, and join it to a prostitute? Never! And don't you realize that if a man joins himself to a prostitute, he becomes one body with her? For the Scriptures say, 'The two are united into one.' But the person who is joined to the Lord is one spirit with him. Run from sexual sin! No other sin so clearly affects the body as this one does. For sexual immorality is a sin against your own body."*

I know that for some of you, this concept of your body, sex, and attachment may be a new one, but it's a very powerful truth. If you have been promiscuous, and you consider your own history, you know, or will see, that this is true. You may not agree with or understand what Paul is talking about in that Scripture passage as it relates to Jesus Christ, but you get the point about joining with a "prostitute," or any woman that is not your wife. Your wife is the only one with whom you should have sex. And you don't have to be a Bible scholar to understand that last verse, number 18, about sexual sin having an unusual, unique, and profound impact on your body. Does the definition of sexual integrity begin to make sense to you now? *Sexually uncorrupted, sound, uncompromised, unimpaired, and complete.*

Sexual promiscuity is to our lives as scotch tape is to paper. It is connected, and doesn't come off without doing damage and fundamentally changing both the tape and the paper. Then you try to use that tape on another piece of paper, and so on. If you're the paper, tape tries to attach to you, but there is less and less good paper to attach to. Spiritually, this is a violent thing to the soul of a person. Is it any wonder that we see so many issues in marriage today, so much infidelity? If your son has formed the habit of being promiscuous before marriage, or his wife has, those tendencies don't go away with the exchange of words and a ring. This is to say nothing of the perversion to which sexual promiscuity opens our boys' minds and bodies. This perverts what good sex really is all about.

If you were promiscuous in the years before you were married, you know what I'm talking about. You know it's real; now you know why. There's no arguing this point, men. If you have not had that experience, and your only sexual partner has been your wife, good for you, because in truth, most men would be envious. I wish that were my story, because this is one of the things on which you don't get "Do Overs"!

Also, if you have a daughter, as I do, you become very mindful of what kind of boys and young men are out there. Clara, my thirteen-year-old daughter, and I were running an errand one day, and there was a car in front of us with a teenager driving it. His license plate said, "My other ride is your daughter." I want to know that there are young men out there who are not predators and poachers, trying to get my daughter. I want to know that there are young men out there who value sexual integrity, and the sexual integrity of girls and women they should be protecting, not poaching.

A BETTER WAY

That is why, in God's plan and purpose for sex, one partner, our mate, is the only person with whom we were intended to experience sex. In both Genesis, chapter 2, verse 24, and again in Matthew, chapter 19 and verse 5, the Bible says: *"A man leaves his father and mother and is joined to his wife, and the two are united into one."* Another translation says, *"The two become one flesh"* (NKJV). This is a serious matter with great implications.

Maybe, as a man, you didn't have sexual integrity, but you have a chance with your boys, to raise boys who have sexual integrity and enter into marriage with a woman who has sexual integrity. They bring their whole sexual being into the relationship with no attachments, no mental baggage, and obviously, no physical consequences. They get to experience each other clean and pure, and that is good!

Just in case you're wondering, they *are* out there – men and women marrying in their mid and late twenties who have sexual integrity. I've known many of them since I began following God. I've had the benefit of conducting marriages for a few of them, and it has absolutely inspired me and given me hope, vision, and motivation in properly training my boys. You can also be inspired and hopeful. You can have the courage to be part of the counterculture and raise a real man preserved for his one wife, a man who only wants a woman who has sexual integrity. Set your boys up for a lifetime of success in their sexual relationship within marriage. One man, one woman, one way!

My boys and I spend time going through a book called *Every Young Man's Battle*,[1] by Stephen Arterburn and Fred Stoeker. This deals directly with the issues of real-world sexual temptation. It is a great springboard into every conceivable conversation about sex: sexual integrity, masturbation, petting and other pseudo-sexual activities, our thought life, the appetite of our eyes, safe-sex myths, pornography, and most importantly, the character of the man that maintains sexual integrity. You must get your boys early on this one, because trust me when I tell you the world and our culture have it out for them right now! I educate my boys on how normal it is to have sexual thoughts and feelings, but that they are not simply animals running on instinct. They are intelligent beings, given something that no other creature on the planet has: free will. They get to say "yes" or "no." They have a choice.

When I say the culture has it out for them I mean it! Marketing says teen sex is okay, and teen-targeted television shows tell them that it's not only okay, but also beautiful and natural. Predators are hunting for your kids on the Internet; there is Internet pornography on the computer and available through mobile devices. How many of your kids have unfiltered access on their mobile devices over which you have no control? How many of you have checked these to see what they have been looking at? My younger son, Brendan, recently got a Twitter account, and he received a random spam communication from someone who wanted to "follow him" on Twitter. It was so raunchy and disgusting that I cannot repeat what it said in this book. Would he have acted on it? I don't think so. But he would have seen it, read it, and been exposed to it. Then there is the drug and alcohol culture in the partying scene that young teens are exposed to and involved in. It's as if your son is in a minefield. He's at one end of the field, and his sexual integrity is on the other side. There are literally hundreds of mines hidden from sight, each one with the potential to take him out or permanently impair him. And it only takes one!

I also talk to my sons about their future mates now. It is a simple question to get them thinking, and it's this: When you get married, do you want your wife to have had sex with other men, or would you prefer that no one else but you has touched and experienced that exclusive part of your wife? The answer is obvious to any man. The next question is simply this: Do you want to be the one to take that exclusive, unique, and precious gift a woman has? Remember, she is someone else's future wife. Do you want to be the one that takes the one and only first-time experience intended by God exclusively for one woman and one man in marriage that bonds them together like no other experience? This is a one-time shot for her; she can never have that physiological and emotional experience back, ever!

When I was young, I sure didn't think like that. But I was never taught to, I was never educated properly, I wasn't even given a chance really to choose. But my boys are another story, and yours can be, also.

PERSONAL ASSESSMENT - SPOKE #4: SEXUAL INTEGRITY

1. Take an inventory of where you are personally.
   - Home Run – Why? What evidence is there?
   - Base Hit – Why? What evidence is there?
   - Strike Out – Why? What evidence is there?

2. What do you have to teach your son, either from doing it well or doing it wrong?
   - Where have you been successful, and what can you teach your son?
   - Where have you missed it, and what can you teach your son about it (what have you learned)?

3. What, if any, personal adjustments do you need to make to model well for your son?

    - As you assess your life currently against this spoke, Sexual Integrity, what needs to change in your life in order for there to be integrity with yourself and your son as you teach him to live well in this spoke?

4. What resources do you need to equip your son in this area that either reinforce your success, or may augment where you may be lacking personally?

    - Search out resources and teaching tools; books, classes, videos, seminars, mentors, etc., that either help illustrate and support your strength here, or augment your weakness and create a strength in both you and your son.

Tip: This is the one area where you cannot recover from some missteps. But you can learn from them and teach your son well. You may need to consider how your own relationship with your wife began, and maybe consider apologizing to her for not conducting yourself with integrity with her and doing it right. I suggest you find great male role models across the age spectrum who have been successful with this spoke. Expose your son to these men, let him hear from them, and talk with them. Use your life as a stark contrast (if it is) to the proper way to do things concerning sexuality. There are excellent resources to help you teach and reinforce healthy principles in regard to sexuality. The Bible will be a rich resource for you here, as with all areas, but in this area, particularly, there is much to be said.

5th SPOKE: PEOPLE
DEVELOPING RELATIONSHIPS

Speak ill of no man, but speak all the good you know of everybody.

– Benjamin Franklin

THE PEOPLE PRINCIPLE

How to win friends and influence people, as Dale Carnegie so famously put it. There is a reality that you won't go far or do much without other people. It is said that a truly wealthy man is one with many friends. It's not all about friends, either. There are people in your life, many of them from which you will want good favor and positive affection, but won't be friends in the traditional, close sense. We sometimes call these people "acquaintances." Life is made up of close intimate friends, friends, acquaintances, and occasional encounters.

BE LIKEABLE – CONSIDER THE ALTERNATIVE

You need all of these people in your life, and people will come and go, in and out of these categories. Regardless, you will want to be in the good graces of all of these people, and why not? Really, if you have a choice to be in a positive, neutral, or negative position with people, why wouldn't you choose the positive? As a leader, a parent, a spouse, a friend, or a peer, you must be likeable. That is not to say that people will like you all of the time, nor should they. But people (spouse, kids, people at work, in your community, at church, etc.) won't want to be around you, much less follow you, if they don't like you. How important is it simply to be liked?

The Golden Rule probably comes to mind: *Do unto others, as you would have them do unto you.* The Golden Rule, as found in the Bible, is defined in this most important commandment of God according to Jesus, Luke, chapter 6, verse 31: *"Love your neighbor as you love yourself."* I think that as you read this book and consider your own life, you will agree that life is indeed easier when people like you. Now, motivation matters, and we will talk about that later; you don't simply apply the commands of the Bible for your personal benefit. However, people are more inclined to help you, to go out of their way for you, and to speak favorably of you when they like you. Really, you have to wonder what went wrong with us as people that someone had to write a book about this subject for us to try to get it right again. Does anyone have to tell you that you like to be around likeable people? Therefore, if you want likeable people to be around you…you might want to try being likeable!

For example, think of someone whom you really like. If that person needed something, wouldn't you be willing to do whatever you could to help them? Wouldn't you make personal sacrifices for them? Don't you speak favorably of them and extend their good reputation to strangers? How would you like those benefits? It doesn't happen by accident.

Granted, some people just seem to have a good disposition and it comes easier for them. Most of us didn't get the "people just like me" gene in our DNA; we have to work at it. But it's well worth it. Most young people don't learn (and many adults have never learned) this early enough; we acquire poor habits in relationship development, not thinking about the importance of the long-term implications of not knowing and applying good relationship skills. Steve Jobs, one of the founders and the former CEO and Chairman of Apple, was a famously bad boss.[1] He was reported to be a most caustic and unlikeable man at times; he was a deplorable manager of people, and it's well-documented. Yet, in spite of his extraordinarily bad behavior with people, he had a very successful company. Two questions beg to be asked, from my perspective:

1. What could his company have been if he had not been so self-centered in his behavior, and had been better with people?
2. What would his legacy be if he had not only created an incredible company, but had also built incredible and

enduring relationships, and left a positive emotional legacy with the people who worked for him?

I know many a person who, because of their position of power, is never forced to mature in this area, and they continue to behave badly because they can. How unfortunate for them!

As a kid, no big deal, but as you enter into adolescence and adulthood, it really begins to matter. Most people will not have the opportunity to have the kind of power and influence as, say, a Steve Jobs which allow them the option to be a poor people-person. Aren't you glad for that? And what an unfortunate loss for those people who never get the fullness of all the rich rewards that come from an abundance of good relationships. You want the positive feelings coming toward you from your parents, teachers, employer, and others in your life. Think about it from this perspective: if it was time for your eulogy, and your friends and family were talking about you, what kind of person would you want them to talk about? A cranky, cantankerous person that didn't seem to get along with anyone, a genuinely nice guy that people loved and got along with well, or an exceptional person who seemed to make friends everywhere; people loved to be around him and always felt better for having spent time with him. Now is the time to choose.

BE RIGHT OR BE HAPPY

This is not complicated, but as I like to say, it's simple, just not easy. Like most everything in life, if you develop the correct habits, everything is easier. It's when you develop unprofitable or poor habits that you have to change; now you have your work cut out for you. It's much easier to develop the right habits first, rather than change bad ones. A friend of mine was fond of saying, "Practice doesn't make perfect; practice makes permanent. Perfect practice makes perfect."

I was once asked, *"Do you want to be right or do you want to be happy"?* You might initially ask, "What does one have to do with the other"? Our demand to be "right" is often at the root of our difficulty in relationships. Right may win the fight, but you lose the battle. A demand to be right leaves someone a loser, and the person who loses doesn't forget easily. The reality that they were wrong does not usually lead to humility and graciousness. On the contrary, it can often leave the person feeling bitter toward you. On the issue of being right, I believe that if you were to honestly analyze the times that you found yourself defending your right to be right, you would probably find, as most do, that it really wasn't a significant matter. It is usually more a case of being caught in the moment and emotion, and the natural tendency is to not be wrong, so we fight to be right. After a while, the issue isn't even the issue.

There are many times that I have blown a perfectly good evening with my wife. We were heading in a great direction for the evening (if you know what I mean), and some little thing came up, not even an important thing, necessarily, and we didn't agree. Rather than just letting it go, I had to prove that I was right. So in my quest to be right, and occasionally proving that I was right, I lost big time! The evening took on an entirely different direction; I was right, for sure…all by myself! Ever been there, men?

I've done the same thing in other relationships, and even in business relationships. Now, we might get more sophisticated and clever in our jousting, but the goal is still the same. When someone wins and someone loses, you run the risk of losing a relationship every time. Back to the story of the ruined evening; I have learned to keep a goal in mind. My goal is a great evening with my wife, and ending it well. If I keep that goal in mind, it easily overrides my tendency to argue my point and win the battle of who's right, regardless of the subject. I have an important goal. I get into trouble when I lose sight of the goal and get caught up in the moment. It is helpful to remember that every person has a unique set of circumstances, experiences, attitudes, etc., and oftentimes the issue isn't a right or wrong thing; it's just a different perspective.

Another relationship killer is sarcasm. I'm not one of those guys that say, *"No sarcasm."* I have a lot of fun with my buddies, and my boys, with a little sarcastic wit and fun. On the other hand, I also recognize that a) not everybody has good self-worth and can play the game, and b) it can cross the line to become a habit, and your entire relationship (or all your relationships) becomes based on sarcasm. Remember this sage advice about sarcasm: The axe forgets, but the tree remembers. At its worst, it can cause irreparable harm to a relationship, depending on the individual, and you may not even realize that you have made an enemy…until it's too late.

RELATIONSHIP ACCOUNTING

Every relationship should have a goal – at a minimum to add value to the other person and have a positive experience, leaving them better than when you found them. On the other end of the spectrum, the goal is to have reciprocal, positive, influential relationships, and garner the warm regard and best intentions of others. Remember, the things that really matter in a successful life require the willing support and help of others, not the involuntary, begrudging assistance of others.

If you have this insatiable hunger to ensure everything is correct, right, and proper (by your definition, by the way), you likely have other emotional issues or insecurities you need to address. Who in their right mind would sabotage their success in life in order to win an argument that, at the end of the day, doesn't really make any difference to anyone after the moment has passed? It's better to be happy than right. You have heard the phrase, *don't cut off your nose to spite your face.* This is a term that was coined after nuns in a monastery cut off their noses, when Vikings raided them in the 9th century, in an effort to intentionally disfigure themselves in order to avoid losing their virginity. Don't do the same thing in your relationships; don't permanently damage your reputation and relationships for the sake of being right. Keep good accounts in your relationships. If you feel so strongly about a point, pull back, count the potential cost, and ask yourself, *"Is it worth having a winner and a loser? How much do I value this relationship?"*

HOW TO WIN FRIENDS AND INFLUENCE PEOPLE

I have had my boys read the legendary and timeless book *How To Win Friends and Influence People*[2], by Dale Carnegie, and we revisit it regularly. I think it is absolutely one of the most important relationship books, leadership books, and sources of wisdom available. If you are a husband, a dad, a friend, a leader, a businessperson, or a volunteer, you will benefit from its principles. Another great work on this subject is *Becoming a Person of Influence*[3], by John Maxwell. I believe that the repetition and applied use of the principles will bear significant benefit in my boys' lives. They will be better husbands, better fathers, better leaders, and better friends as a result. They will have much more success in life, regardless of how success is defined. Applying the tools of developing good relationships is like greasing the skids of life; it's just easier, smoother, and life requires less effort.

As I said earlier, practice makes permanent, but perfect practice makes perfect. While your boys are still young train them properly and they will do much better. Imagine how your son will stand out in the crowd of other young men when he has these skills and attitudes. He will win the gracious favor of those who will have some influence over his success in life. How much more peaceable and enjoyable will his home be! How much better will life be, in general, simply by greasing the cogs and making it a point to have good relationships!

This is one of the hardest components to communicate, teach, and apply with my sons. At their young ages, they didn't get it. It's all theory to them at 13. I have to put this subject in terms they can understand and that are relevant to them. It is not easy going back to a 13, 14, 15, or 16-year-old's world at age 45. The additional challenge is that teenagers have an uncanny ability, a gift really, to cause us, as parents, to abandon all these awesome people skills. They have a way of causing me to go from the How to Win Friends poster child to nearly being eligible for a Most Wanted poster in the Post Office, all in the blink of an eye. So with the boys, I give grace; I am human, also. Though, practically speaking, I coach them on how to use the principles with their mom, with their siblings, and with their teachers. Trust me; they will come to you often when they don't get their way with one of those parties just mentioned. These are fantastic coaching moments to help them re-evaluate motives and strategies to try again. I let them know honestly, though, that there are plenty of times, even when going back again after you have not handled a situation well, you will still be unsuccessful in getting what you want.

Often these are one-shot opportunities, so the lesson is to get it right the first time. My boys have personally seen the benefit of this process when they are conscious enough to apply it with their mother and sister and others. However, because they have both read the book, and because they are ornery boys, they will make it hard on each other when they try to use the principles with each other…but that's a good lesson, as well, plus it's a lot of fun to watch. Finally, and maybe the most challenging part, is that it causes me to be a far better parent. It forces me to use these principles with my sons and others, rather than just telling them what I want them to do. So I do my best to lead by example, and that is, at times, neither expedient nor fun, but it's a great personal challenge, and it's a great way to condition them in how to act.

Regarding dealing with people, there are some fundamental principles I have extrapolated from Dale Carnegie's book in order to give you some things to think about as to the importance of this section, and to help you set your son up for success:

- Always leave people feeling better about themselves than when they saw you.
- Always listen more than you talk, and ask questions.
- Always make eye contact and be fully present.
- Always remember their name.
- Always remember little details about them and their life, and ask about those little details.
- Always seek the good of others above your own personal gain.
- Always be genuinely interested in other people.
- Always be patient with people.

You could compile your own list, or take this one and add to it, but remember, keep the main thing the main thing, *"Do unto others as you would have them do unto you."* Pretty simple, really, it's just not easy. But remember, you will sow what you reap, the law of reciprocity.

Always leave people feeling better about themselves. People are walking wounded, for the most part. They have been hit by friendly fire, and they are often gun shy when it comes to people. Most people are hurt at some level, and as my pastor is fond of saying, *hurting people hurt people.* So when you are the one person that someone meets in the course of a day, and you make them feel better about themselves, you are golden! And you have done a good thing. They will not necessarily remember what you said, but they will remember how you made them feel. I read in a book, *Fierce Conversations*[4] by Susan Scott, about how we leave an emotional wake behind us. Leave positive emotional wakes behind you. Emotion is the glue that creates "truth" in our minds about people. If you create an overpowering positive emotional experience with someone, they would be hard pressed to allow you to be spoken ill of in their presence. So make sure that people have a positive emotional experience with you.

Always listen more than you talk. I've heard it over and over again; it's why God gave us two ears and one mouth. I don't know if that was a divine message we have missed, or simply because he knew we'd look stupid with one ear and two mouths…but it works for this principle. It has been said that the best conversationalists are the best listeners. So be quiet, listen, and learn. I would suggest that if you were in a 10-minute conversation with someone and you listened well, listened actively, stayed present in the conversation, asked a few questions, and made affirmative nods and comments, you would be heralded as a most sincere person who really cares. Your stock would go up exponentially with that individual, and you really said nothing. Listening is the way we learn, because everything we say we already know. How else are you going to learn if you don't listen? When you talk, you only share what you already know. People don't want to hear nearly as much as they want to be heard. Another very important lesson is this: how well a person listens is largely based on how well they were listened to. Remember, people don't care how much you know until they know how much you care. So listen well.

Always be present. Part of listening effectively is remaining present in the conversation, and that is a discipline. People are so used to others looking around, acknowledging others, pausing the conversation to say something to someone else, losing eye contact, and being MIA. This is a growing problem today as shorter and shorter attention spans are being developed with instant communication tools that don't require us to be "present." This behavior is a value statement to the other person. The message they receive is, "I don't value you." When they actually experience someone that makes them the center of the universe for the moment, they are shocked, surprised, and delighted. You are the standout. When you are present, you are communicating something very powerful; you are saying, *"You are all that matters to me right now."* There are few things that are more esteeming and emotionally cauterizing than being present. People know when you aren't; they are used to it, since they do it themselves. Consequently, they strongly sense when you are present. This is a small, but significant, tool in dealing with people.

Always remember their name. I was in sales for many years, and one of the fundamental principles taught, and, unfortunately, it was for the purpose of manipulation, was remembering people's names. Dale Carnegie said that the sweetest sound to anyone's ear is the sound of his or her own name, and it's true; it's another small, yet powerful, truth. It's easier for some and more difficult for others. But it's worth the effort to learn some techniques. Plus, if you have ever needed to remember someone's name that is important to you for some reason, and you cannot remember their name, it's awkward and frustrating, and you spend way too much time trying to avoid the obvious to figure it out. But when you remember their name, it's like a beautiful bell sounding in their ear, ringing just the right notes to cause a smile to come upon their face.

165

And you did it.

Always remember little details. People expect you to remember the big things; they are shocked and surprised when you remember the little things. No one is expecting that, and it will separate you from the average. I will never forget a friend of mine telling me once, as I asked about a little detail about something he shared in regard to his wife, *"Allen, you are the only person that asks about that, and I really appreciate it."* It was sincere, as was my question about his wife. And it separated me from the pack. Remembering the small details demonstrates that you really are listening and you really care.

Always seek the best good for others above your own. Your motives matter, so this should be high up on everyone's list. I mentioned earlier, regarding always remembering names, that I was trained in that technique for sales, but it was not because it was a good thing to do, rather it was because it helped me close sales. The motive for your actions must be pure; people will smell a fake. You have all been around someone who is clearly not authentic and is self-serving. You have also been around someone who was genuinely interested in you. There is a sharp contrast between the two, and it's obvious. There are different spirits behind authentic and manufactured. You can employ all the techniques listed, and if people sense you're not authentic, it's all for nothing.

Always be genuinely interested in other people. It's easy to be genuinely interested in people because people are interesting. Everyone is unique and different, and interesting in all sorts of ways. The more you get to know someone, and the more you ask questions and explore who they are, the more you become genuinely intrigued by them. It's easy and irresponsible to simply indulge someone to get through a conversation. The fact is that a conversation is taking place, so you might as well engage. Make it a goal to find out something genuinely unique and interesting about each new person you talk with. As I mentioned earlier, people are used to being marginalized, and unfortunately, some much more than others. Develop the authentic desire to explore the people around you and you will make a world of discoveries. There is more to the people around you than you realize. The challenge that we have here is two-fold. One is that we don't take the time necessary to be interested, and two, there are people that we don't want to indulge because we don't think they have anything to offer and, thus, are not a good use of our time. Aren't you glad God and your parents don't think like that? Simply recall how it makes you feel when someone takes a genuine interest in you, and realize that you can give the same gift to someone else.

Always be patient with people. Admittedly, my biggest challenge! The other things mentioned in this key are much easier if you will simply be patient with people. People come with all sorts of experiences, attitudes, and quirks. You have no idea, generally, what a person has experienced or been through. After many hours in counseling with people, I have come to understand that most have been through some pretty dramatic stuff in life, and it has an effect. People are not born different (although unique); they are made different by their experiences in life. Neither do you know what a person is experiencing when you meet them. There may be crisis in their life, and it's creating an enormous amount of stress. People often don't do their best under stress. I remember meeting an individual years ago for the first time. The first impression was memorable, but for all the wrong reasons! It was the kind of encounter that makes you say, "If I ever see him again, it will be too soon." Looking back, I'm ashamed that I shared my encounter with others and spoke unfavorably about this person. Not long after, I discovered he was under a lot of stress financially and had just found out his wife was leaving him that morning. I didn't get him at his best, but I got the best he had to offer at that moment. That day, I learned a lesson about being patient with people. Remember the Golden Rule: do unto others what you would have them do unto you.

SET THEM UP FOR SUCCESS

One of the most significant benefits of all this is that, as your sons learn these techniques and develop this skill, their influence will increase and their opinion will matter. It's a funny little paradox, but as you effectively subordinate your opinion, it suddenly takes on significance and is sought after; your sons must learn this truth about people if they are to have effective, influential relationships.

As we wrap up this chapter, remember why we are talking about this subject. Give your boys the very best chance to succeed in life, to be fully prepared to leave the nest and strike out on their own. When they leave, they will need people more than ever in college, in career, in work, and in relationships. Their need for effective relationships, develop friends and admirers, and to influence others will go up exponentially when they leave your protection. We don't do anything significant alone, so the ability to win friends and influence others is a critical skill for your son to develop as he becomes a man. It's worth reminding you again, as we close, what Dale Carnegie said so many years ago: *"People don't care how much you know until they know how much you care."*

A closing thought. Some have said that *How to Win Friends and Influence People* is about sucking up, brown-nosing, or manipulating. I would simply say that those people have probably not read the book. The premise of the book is a sincere and authentic desire to know, care, and serve other people, and you will simply reap what you sow. It is naïve to think that you can bypass the necessary skills for developing healthy relationships at all levels and be effective in your life. If you are even remotely successful in your relationships with others, you are probably already applying the principles of Dale Carnegie's book.

Personal Assessment - Spoke #5: People

1. Take an inventory of where you are personally.
   - Home Run – Why? What evidence is there?
   - Base Hit – Why? What evidence is there?
   - Strike Out – Why? What evidence is there?

2. What do you have to teach your son, either from doing it well or doing it wrong?
   - Where have you been successful, and what can you teach your son?
   - Where have you missed it, and what can you teach your son about it (what have you learned)?

3. What, if any, personal adjustments do you need to make to model well for your son?
   - As you assess your life currently against this spoke, People, what needs to change in your life in order for there to be integrity with yourself and your son as you teach him to live well in this spoke?

4. What resources do you need to equip your son in this area that either reinforce your success, or may augment where you may be lacking personally?
   - Search out resources and teaching tools: books, classes,

videos, seminars, mentors, etc. that either help illustrate and support your strength here, or augment your weakness and create a strength in both you and your son.

Tip: I don't know of a better resource, although it's dated, than How to Win Friends and Influence People. *Also look for other men you admire who seem to just naturally attract people, those men that people seem to just like. Who are the men in your life that you just seem naturally inclined to follow? I am talking about the people who are truly authentic and seem to genuinely care about other people, and you see this has contributed to their success. I made a point of finding these men in my life, and in my sons' lives, and I used them as illustrations of how important this spoke is to having a quality, successful life, to see how much better life is when people like you and are your fans.*

6th SPOKE: MONEY OUR ACHILLES' HEEL

Money is only a tool. It will take you wherever you wish, but it will not replace you as the driver.

– Ayn Rand

AN ILLUSIVE STRENGTH

An Achilles' Heel is a potentially deadly weakness that, in spite of overall strength, can actually lead to our downfall. Money, if not properly managed and kept in perspective, has the potential to be your downfall, no matter how strong you may be in other areas of your life. Achilles was thought to be a great warrior, with only one area of vulnerability, and ironically, he did not know it was a weakness until it brought him down. Ignorance can come with a high price; ignorance about money can cost you everything.

You've all heard the statement: *Money is the root of all evil.* That's not an accurate recitation. It is from the Bible in 1 Timothy, chapter 6, verse 10, and it actually says, *"The LOVE of money is the root of all evil."* Money is simply a tool, and can be constructive and build something, or destructive and destroy something…a building, a person, a family, a community, etc. With a healthy attitude, it's a means to an end, and nothing more.

This subject fell into the all-important list of topics for my sons' rites of passage because, maybe more than anything else, the issue of money – more specifically, the understanding, appreciation, and management of money (called stewardship) – caused me a lot of pain. Money is an excellent slave, but an extremely poor master. And unfortunately today, maybe more than at any other time in history, people are enslaving themselves to money. This is happening for several reasons: greed, selfishness, self-gratification, lack of self-discipline, search for fulfillment, lack of goals and vision, lack of education (ignorance) and training, and poor role models (from home to government, to business, to sports).

THE CURRENT SITUATION

Before I get started, let's take a quick snapshot of our current situation:

- Our economy in the U.S. is almost entirely driven by consumption. We are, for the most part, no longer a manufacturing economy, or at best, we are only a shadow of what we once had been. We actually produce very little of anything that we consume. We have become a largely retail and service economy. If people are buying stuff, a lot of it and all the time, then businesses are making money.
- Companies have become masterful at enticing you, drawing you, and manipulating you. They spend billions of dollars each year in understanding how to "get you," and to appeal to the weakest part of you. We will hear over and over again, either directly or indirectly, *"You deserve it."* We are constantly influenced by a culture controlled by media and money that makes us feel inferior if we don't have the latest gadget, the coolest TV, the nicest car, and so on.
- Forty years ago, credit didn't exist. Our society was a cash society. Many of the companies that want your money today, and offer you credit, would have thought that to be a "sinful" practice. Within a very, very short period of time, we have gone from a primarily cash-basis society to a completely indebted society that has, a) normalized debt, and b) in fact, thinks something is wrong with you if you don't have debt.
- In that same period of time, we have generally lost all sense of delayed gratification, and there has been a fundamental shift in the definition of "need."

The change in attitude toward credit, accompanied by the "got to have it now" and "got to have it all" attitudes, have coalesced to create a dynamic that has dramatically changed our culture and our society.

HAVE OR HAVE NOT, THAT IS NOT THE QUESTION

So just to get it out of the way, I like money. I like lots of money. I enjoy having things; things are nice. We can say all we want about the "evils" of money, but life sure seems a lot easier when you have plenty of it. A good friend of mine is fond of saying that he has had no money, and he has quite a lot of money, and he prefers having money. Life seems to be a lot more challenging when you don't have much. This chapter isn't about being a miser, or being a "hater" on those who have a lot. I have had much and I have had little, and as the Apostle Paul said (in A.D. 30, this is not a new problem by the way) in Philippians, chapter 4, verse 11, *"In both states I have learned to be content,"* though it's a little nicer having some money, that is, as long as it does not have you!

One thing is for sure, I don't want my boys to be slaves to money; it is an extremely poor master. I don't want them to put themselves, or their families, in those shackles, and trust me when I say it feels every bit as real as being chained and shackled; you may already know this from your personal experience. I don't want my boys to go through what I went through, and I don't want them to drag their families through what I was dragged through, and what I have dragged my family through.

We must be careful here, though. The reason being, with a little root cause analysis we discover something interesting. The issues and challenges of money, or finances, aren't really about the money or finances at all. We could spend all our time treating a symptom and never deal with the real problem, and, consequently, never solve the issue. The issues and challenges of money and finances are about you and your attitudes, habits, and disciplines, not money itself. You see, I know people who don't make a lot of money by most standards, but they are doing well: sending kids to college, buying their house, going to dinner, going on vacations, and they have peace in their home. I also know people who are making a lot of money who are barely eking by and are under enormous stress.

The key to being successful financially is found in your attitudes toward money and your subsequent behaviors. It is what you do with what you have that determines more than anything else how much you will have. As Jesus himself said in Matthew, chapter 25, verse 21, *"To him who is faithful with little, he will be given more. But to him who has been unfaithful, what he has will be taken away."* Like it or not, this is a principle that I have both observed and participated in, and you can't deny it. The consequences are sometimes delayed, but they are not denied.

When I was a kid growing up, we didn't have a lot of stuff. Christmases would be big gift-giving times. We had a little recreation place on the ocean in Washington where we went on occasion, we had some toys, and so on. But there was an enormous amount of stress in our home. As a kid, I didn't always get it, but as I grew older, I realized it was about money. My dad and mom both worked; they had to, to support the debt created and the lifestyle pursuit. And it seemed that no matter how much they worked, there still wasn't enough. As a child, it always seemed to me like others had more than us, and the stress around money was intense. I didn't realize it at the time, but most of the people around us that I envied were making the same mistakes and crawling into the same financial pit.

THE STRESS TEST

There were eventually some pretty dramatic financial consequences for our family. There is no doubt in my mind that the money stuff contributed to the divorces we experienced as kids. It was sure the source of a lot of fighting. Now that I am a husband and a dad, I have a lot of empathy for my parents. Raising a family and taking care of a family can be very hard, and very expensive, and I had the same issues as my parents. Money caused a lot of stress in my marriage(s), or rather the poor handling of it, and was, no doubt, a big contributor to my subsequent divorces.

Money is very similar to a gun. You hear people say that guns kill, however, guns are simply objects; they only become good or bad in the hands of a person. Money is the same way; it's just an object, and it does good or ill only once it's in someone's hands. Money as with a gun, if not handled responsibly can do a lot of unintentional harm, purely out of ignorance or accident by the handler. Until that point, it is a neutral element. There are few things, if anything, like money that will expose our weaknesses. For example, if there is a crack in cement, when it's nice and warm outside, you may not even see it; the crack closes up as it expands from the warmth. I know this is true because I observed this in some concrete in my back yard around my pool. When it's warm outside, the concrete expands and you can't even tell there is a crack. But when winter comes and it begins to get cold, the concrete contracts and the crack appears. Cold weather causes the crack to appear. Money and financial pressures are very similar. You may have cracks in your marriage, in your character, or in your soul, and money can be the cold weather that will cause them to open up.

Remember the statement I quoted earlier about the love of money? At the end of the day, that's the problem. You see, we live in a society that has gotten progressively more self-indulgent, money-hungry, and materialistic. We have come to a place where things that were once "wants" are now classified as "needs." And we may not consider that we don't want more money; we just want more and more of what money can buy. Money is just a means.

MODERN-DAY PHENOMENON

Like other areas of this book, a little historical context is necessary. If we remove ourselves from the lessons and experiences of the past, we have no context for the place we find ourselves. We would just naturally think that our lives, struggles, and desires are normal. Not true. I referenced a great book earlier by Tom Brokaw, *The Greatest Generation*. What we don't realize is that we live in unprecedented times for America, as far as prosperity and what we think we deserve. Very few living today in America really have any true idea of sacrifice and lack. This is profoundly evident when we see what qualifies a person as "poor" today. A person today will be poor by government standards and still have cell phones, flat panel televisions, cable TV, and the like.

I am in no way making light of people authentically in need and struggling. But what I am trying to do is provide some context. Go back 70 or 80 years ago to the Depression and World War II and you'll see for yourself how our definition of "need" has changed. Remember the Lees? They lived through the Great Depression, World War II and subsequent times of challenge. If you don't know anyone over 80, or have not had a good, long conversation with them about how they grew up, and their life, you have missed an enormous opportunity.

ONE MAN'S STORY – A THROWBACK

I introduced you briefly to Norm Lee in the preface. He grew up during the Depression in Iowa, and his parents were poor sharecroppers. He had nothing, quite literally nothing, and that's without exaggeration. But that was not uncommon then. When he was 17, he took everything he had, which fit into one small, modest suitcase, and $20 cash, and took a bus to Oregon where his sister lived. From there he began working in the lumber industry. He was very frugal and resourceful, and coming out of the Depression in the Mid-West, he knew the difference between a need and a want. To make a long story short, when he got his paycheck and money in his hand, because he was disciplined, and had goals and motivation, he began investing in building small homes, in real estate, etc. He was not a man prone to chase easy money ideas and schemes; he didn't believe in those things. He was traditional in his values and mindset about money. Earn it honestly, earn it in a fair way, but you earn it. Something that isn't earned, a price paid for it, isn't valued.

By the time I met them 30 years ago, the Lees were quite wealthy, but I didn't know it. They lived modestly. Their youngest son was my best friend, and he drove an old car that had been handed down from his parents. They could have easily purchased him a new car at 16 as we tragically see so many parents do today. They never purchased new cars, always only used vehicles for cash, although they could have walked into any luxury car show room and paid cash without blinking. They live in the same house today that they built and paid cash for 30 years ago. It's a nice house, but modest for their abilities. Mr. Lee works on his own house when things break down. They don't wear expensive designer clothes or accessories. There are no trappings of wealth around or on them.

Today, they are very well-to-do with not a financial worry in the world. They are in a position to do wonderful things and help people in need. However, they will not do for people what they can do for themselves. They know how easy it is to weaken a human being with money. I had the tremendous opportunity to know them when I was younger, but I didn't glean any of their wisdom. Later, when I had made a mess of things, I approached them for advice and counsel. They never offered unsolicited advice. It wasn't their style, and they knew it was a waste of their time and energy. They gave me great, timeless advice then, but I didn't like what I heard. So rather than buckling down and disciplining myself, and heeding their council, I creatively tried to solve my problems, all to no avail. I may have gotten out of a bit of a mess momentarily, but I didn't develop any of the attitudes and character traits they espoused as necessary to stay out of a mess, so I simply recreated my messes. It wasn't until years later that I finally began to apply their wisdom.

If it was difficult to get through to a 20-something then about self-discipline, delayed gratification, long-term planning, and financial stewardship, it's much more difficult today. This is simply because as a society, where we did not value those things 20 years ago, the pendulum has only swung farther away from those basic common sense values and ideas today. The reasons for this have already been articulated in the book's previous chapters so I won't go into them again. But the things that caused my friend to have a durable and sustainable wealth, a quality life, and financial peace are still the same principles required today. Some things truly are timeless. They may not be romantic or exciting, but they work. As we delay embracing them because they demand us to be disciplined, there will be a price to pay. Today, I only wish I could turn back the clock those 30 years, and apply the wisdom and advice that was readily available to me then. Oh, how my life would be different today!

That window is closing rapidly with time, and I suggest if you don't have an 80-year-old or older friend, get one quick. Buy them coffee, sit with them, ask a few questions, and listen, listen, listen. You will learn much. Somewhere along the way since that time, we have lost the lessons they learned, and we have swung dramatically in the opposite direction from frugality and self-control to excess and indulgence.

As parents, we want our kids to have it better than we did. Our parents wanted the same thing for us, and so on down through the years. But that was not always the case. There was a day when parents realized that, by giving their kids too much, they actually hurt them; parents do serious, and sometimes irreparable, harm to them. The pressure on kids and parents these days to have the Ipod, or the Iphone, or the Ipad, or the car, or the clothes, and the pressure on the family to have a boat, or the jet skis, or the quads, the Wii, the Xbox, or the 50" flat panel, can be intense. My boys aren't any different, but I am proud of them, as they have come to understand that, with money, there is always a reckoning, and there is always an exchange.

DELAYED GRATIFICATION – REALLY?

My goal with my sons is to help them make today's financial decisions while keeping tomorrow in mind. If my son wants a $100 pair of jeans today (I still have a hard time with that reality), what is he saying "no" to tomorrow? What will be the things he wants tomorrow (figuratively speaking) that are more important than the things he is so desperately wanting now?

We just went school clothes shopping a couple of weeks ago, and my son, who, much to my chagrin is fashion conscious, saved over the summer, in order to buy a $125 pair of jeans. I tried to calmly, and rationally reason with him to no avail. I did not say "no" to him, I simply did not participate, financially, at all, with his decision. It was difficult to restrain myself, and not simply exercise my authority as his father and say, "no." As we walked out of the store however, with that Buckle bag in hand, he said to me, "Dad, I don't think I'll ever spend that much money on a pair of jeans again." He didn't like parting with that much of his hard earned money, for a pair of jeans; he had some buyer's remorse. Ironically, while in line to pay, there was a mother, arms full, who was encouraging my son with his purchase and fashion sense. She was clueless, as she helped him justify what a good and wise purchase he was making.

This same son of mine was once at a skateboard event. He wanted a skateboard deck badly. The pressure was on, others had new decks, his was old, and the vendors were there with a full court press. He cracked in a moment of weakness and bought a deck he didn't really "need," although he certainly argued for the "need." He called me after he had bought it. I asked him a few questions about the other things we had talked about that he wanted to spend money on in the coming weeks and months. I was so proud of him. After we got off the phone, he went back to the vendor to return the deck. Initially, they didn't want to take it back. He was persistent, found a loophole in their policy, and got his money back. That was a couple of years ago, but he still talks about it today. That is not to say that my kids don't fall prey to the temptation of the short-term desire. But we talk about it, never missing an opportunity to learn.

OUR KIDS ARE PREY – ARE WE COMPLICIT?

Our kids want these things, and why not? Extremely clever marketers (remember Merchants of Cool) feed their appetites at a very young age. The pressure grows as their friends have all the toys, and it's all you hear about from your kids. Parents who don't know any better begin to spoil their kids with these things. They do one of two things most often, not always, but most often. They either borrow and go into debt to appease their children (and their own self-worth), or they jeopardize their future security by using money that should be going into savings, making additional principle payments on a mortgage, college funding, etc. But how they are doing it isn't so much the issue as what they are doing. They are setting an example that their kids are watching. Neither model is responsible for the long-term well-being of the family's financial health. Then we have the family who has all the bases covered. They are wise with their money, and they have the ability to provide nicer things. The question then begs to be asked: "Just because you can, does that mean you should"? I see many parents who compensate for their own lack during their childhood years with their kids now. I know this is true, because I was one of those parents. The questions I would have each parent consider are these:

- What are you conditioning your kids to think of as "normal"?
- What attitudes are they developing about money?
- What appetites are you creating in your kids for material things?
- How will this influence the major decisions in their life ahead (career, marriage, savings)?

You know how hard it is to have something nice, and then have it taken away or you have to give it up. You have probably compromised yourself in some ways that you are not proud of in order to keep things. Do you want to set your boys up for the same thing?

Remember, I said I wasn't a hater, and I'm not. Some people have the means to take care of their family very well, secure the future, and do really cool things for their kids. But many don't, and it's keeping up with those who do that causes trouble. And why do we do that? Although it may often be a sincere desire to bless our kids, our wife, and our family, sometimes it's a lack of leadership and self-control. Sometimes it's a crack deep down in our soul; it's a pride thing, or a feeling of loss in our own life as a child, something we think we missed out on. It's something broken in us that prevents us from having the courage and strength of character to say "*no*" to appeasing the immediate at the expense of the future. It manifests in a lack of self-control – an absolutely essential quality necessary for a man to possess, and pass on to his sons.

OUR ACHILLES' HEEL

As men, we can begin to feel less worthy, or less of a man, less of a dad, and our self-worth and ego take a real hit when we feel like our kids are going without when compared to their friends. We begin to beat ourselves up for not "providing" for our family. So what do we do? We begin to borrow money on credit, use money that should be going into savings, work extra hours or two jobs to buy the "stuff" for our kids and family, or send our wives out to work to maintain a lifestyle that is really about making us feel better about ourselves. There is a financial teacher, author, and educator named Dave Ramsey. He has a syndicated talk show, programs, and a company that helps people get themselves back into financial shape. In Dave's highly regarded book *Financial Peace*[1], and his widely used video based program, *Financial Peace University*[2], he says that where it took our parents 35 years to have certain things in their life, such as a home, new car, and so on, we have all that within seven years of marriage, but at a much higher cost. Two generations ago, debt was unthinkable. One generation ago, it was considered a necessary evil. This generation thinks it's the norm, and we have become slaves to it all in only 40 years! And its roots go back to a lack of self-control, delayed gratification, and/or our own brokenness inside.

The insidious thing about all this is that it's not really about our kids, our wife, and our family having nice things. It's about you and me, and the image and expectations we have set up for ourselves in our mind of what a man, a dad, and husband really is. If our neighbor is buying new cars, new boats, new dirt bikes, a new camper, or going on cool vacations and we aren't, we begin to feel "less than," as a man. Our kids innocently begin commenting on all their friends' cool stuff, telling you all about the vacation they just took to Maui and all the cool things they did. You see your kids less frequently because they might be hanging out at the neighbor's house a little more, since they have all the right video consoles. Or your kids are constantly talking about their friends' Iphone, and on it goes.

You begin to even envy in your heart a little bit (or a lot) as you watch the stuff accumulate. Seriously, who wouldn't? I did. You begin to measure yourself as a provider against other people. Again, the insidious hold that begins to take root is how this is making you feel as a man, based on the scripts our modern culture plays to define what it means to be a man. So what do you do? You begin to feed the beast, but that is one hungry animal that is never quite satisfied. One day you wake up, and you have a world of hurt on you. You have begun to feel the pressure to keep up the payments. You are beginning to fall behind a little here and there. You have to use the credit card for the simple everyday things that should be paid for in cash. You have to work longer, harder, or begin looking for another job to make more money. Your wife may have to begin working, if she isn't already. Anyone who has been to this place knows how quickly you can create the problem, and what a long and painful process it is to get out.

For some, it's not the immediate pressure, because there is plenty of "cash flow," but the cash isn't flowing where it should, and you feel the pressure later when college comes, a crisis comes, or retirement comes. Today, many are feeling immense pressure because of the Economic Crisis, and many who thought they were okay are realizing they aren't. We are seeing many "toys" and things go away; they are missing out of the driveway, they have "for sale" signs on them, the house is empty, and of course, all the retailers are hurting because people aren't buying nearly as much. I believe that what we are experiencing right now, for many, will cause a "reset" to occur in the financial hard drive of their mind. It will be challenging, but it will be good in the end if we come back to our senses, come back to common sense.

There are really two issues here: one is you and your money, and the other is you and your sons. There is one common denominator – you. You must be wise with your money, and understand it is a tool and not a measure of your self-worth. You must also realize that, regardless of what is happening around you in an increasingly indulgent culture, you actually do harm to your kids with the misuse of money and lack of good stewardship, particularly when they associate it with self-worth. As a dad, it might be wise to consider the Hippocratic Oath doctors take concerning patients, but applied to us with our sons – *do no harm.*

THE STAKES ARE HIGH

Dad, let me ask you a question. When you are 60 and your son is 35, what would you think if your grandkids had every toy on the planet, every electronic gadget, your son and his family had nice cars and a big house…but his marriage was disintegrating over the pressure and stress of money? Set your sons up for success by training them correctly now. Help your son now to develop healthy attitudes about money; help him now to develop good financial habits. You may not have done a very good job yourself up to this point, but it's never too late to do the right thing. You may, in fact, be guilty of not leading well in this area. Okay fine, you're guilty. So do you continue on with that behavior? I mentioned this in the area of sexual integrity. If there is any guilt and shame here, let it perform its function, which is to motivate you to do something different. Apologize to those necessary, admit your faults, ask for forgiveness, and make the corrections necessary. But once there, leave the shame and guilt behind. If you hang out on the guilt train you'll be no use to your kids; it will kill your motivation to begin doing the right thing. There is always NOW and an opportunity to do the next right thing.

How could you take a book seriously on the subject of helping a boy become a man and not talk about money? It is the number one cause of marital problems, it's a primary reason people get stuck in life, it is a primary cause people don't experience more in life, and it's a contributing reason people are not fulfilled in life. People kill for it, people die for it, people commit crimes for it, people go to jail for it, relationships are compromised over it, and businesses and lives are ruined over it. But remember, it's only a tool; in the hands of one person it can be harnessed and mastered, and much good can come from it. In the hands of another, it can be a shackle and a master, and much grief can come from it. May I say that I am not writing this chapter from the perspective of the guy who did it right. No, in fact, I am writing this chapter as the guy who did it all wrong. It has been a long road for me to come to the place where I can write this chapter. And I'm still a work in progress. But here's what I know...*you can change.*

FOUNDATIONS IN SAND

Your boys observe, they learn, and they do...most often just as you have done. If you are sitting here right now reading this book and you do not have financial peace, you are creating a legacy for your kids, and maybe your grandkids, that will perpetuate itself. Like everything else in life, we learn by observation, and we tend to repeat what we see. These things are a combination of taught and caught. Your sons must be taught, and then they must see it demonstrated consistently in order for it to be caught. When you left home and went out on your own, did you take the time to educate yourself on how to use money effectively and wisely? Did you read great books by wise people? Did you get a mentor who has done it really well and learn? Did you observe others who had financial peace and say, *"I am going to develop those habits"?* My guess is the answer is, *no, probably not.* Most of us don't. We just go headlong into life with the same habits as our parents – wanting to be different, sometimes with different intentions because we want a different outcome, but with the same or similar habits, with the same or similar results. Remember the definition of insanity: *doing the same thing over and over again and expecting different results.*

I mentioned how my faith had such a powerful influence in my life, and my eyes began to open; I began to get some wisdom and learn the truth about money. Jesus gives a parable about the significance of his teaching and the Bible in Matthew, chapter 7, verses 24-27: *"Anyone who listens to my teaching and follows it is wise, like a person who builds a house on solid rock. Though the rain comes in torrents and the floodwaters rise and the winds beat against that house, it won't collapse because it is built on bedrock. But anyone who hears my teaching and doesn't obey it is foolish, like a person who builds a house on sand. When the rains and floods come and the winds beat against that house, it will collapse with a mighty crash."* I had to learn the hard way that Jesus is right; a life that is built on the wisdom of God's word is solid, secure, and enduring. I started my business, and over time things began to improve. I made better financial decisions. I began leading my family well. I developed the self-discipline to say *no.* More importantly, I developed a healthy self-worth and identity so my sense of value and significance wasn't in what I could buy or give to my family. I no longer had to fill the hole in my soul with stuff, trying to keep up with a cultural norm. I was building my financial house on solid rock.

A decade later, however, after making many good decisions, I began to make less-than-ideal ones. I began to feel a little too secure and confident in my situation, and slowly pride and indulgence began to creep back in. I didn't recognize it at first as it was subtle, but the words I began to use were *"I deserve," "My family deserves,"* etc. Before too long, although not living really extravagantly, but better than many, I began to move my financial house from solid ground and began laying the foundation in sand again. You may not know this, but the Bible actually talks about money more than any single subject, and not about being wealthy as some falsely believe, but rather about being wise, diligent, patient, and above all, trusting in God and not your money. I don't believe it's a coincidence that the thing God chose to speak about most frequently has become potentially our country's largest problem.

HISTORY REPEATS ITSELF

It all seemed just great until the cracks began to appear as the pressure began to be applied. This time it was precipitated by the Economic Crisis of 2008. I hadn't gone crazy, but I had made some decisions that went against the grain of what I had learned and come to understand. I violated my own principles, and the principles in God's word. If you didn't know already, you cannot violate principles without consequences. My motives were good, but I really had not solidly established the character quality of self-control. Rather than keeping my eye on the goal of savings, college, security, and being self-disciplined, I began to acquire a few things when I wasn't truly financially healthy enough for them. My kids had some things, and yes, we did some cool stuff and had nice cars. We didn't initially have any credit card debt or car payments. Rather than being really honest with myself regarding want versus need, I began purchasing new things, cars, etc. I used cash to pay for them, so I had a false sense of responsibility. I rationalized my choices by telling myself that at least I wasn't borrowing money, when, in fact, I should have been putting that money in savings. Eventually, a car payment was created, and slowly, as our business began to deteriorate because of the economy, so my income began to deteriorate, and the credit cards came out.

One by one, the things began to go away, debt began to accumulate, and in no time at all we were in a mess again after having been free. I got the opportunity to relearn all the lessons, reapply all the truths that I have written to you about, and "reset" my own attitudes and habits. And you know what? Although it is not comfortable I am thankful for it. My sons are learning in real time. That is just my story. In my world, I took a quick look around and said, "Not my boys." They will learn better, they will know better, and they will live and lead better; this will not be my final chapter or legacy, and it won't be their heritage.

TEACHABLE MOMENTS

I have a phenomenal wife, by the way; she is my cheerleader, and I have a great relationship with God. My identity is solidly tied to the one who made me, not the world's definition of whether or not I'm successful. I have amazing, balanced, loving kids, so this crisis, while difficult, was not devastating. The other spokes in the wheel were good, and this one, while it has been damaged, was not beyond repair, so the stress of this financial undoing didn't negatively affect my marriage or my family in the really important areas, such as our relationships, our faith, and our values. I can't think of a better example of how a healthy life, how investing in and developing each key area, can seriously mitigate the damage of a bent or broken spoke.

What all this has enabled me to do is to sit back humbly and say, *"What now?"* I can't do much about the current situation I am in, but I will do all I can. And the most important thing I can do is teach my boys well, both from my experience of doing it right, and my experience of doing it wrong (and they participated in both), and how to recover.

As for my boys and their rite of passage, I was very conscious of helping them understand and personally experience the value of money, the purpose of money, the importance of planning, goals, and preparation, the importance of self-control and delayed gratification, the true cost of things, the tangible results, and the consequences of people's decisions in their lives and the lives of others. I taught them about budgeting, and I shared with them what it costs to do things like vacations; I put them in charge of their own money, and let them make mistakes. I would drive them around and we would see the tangible consequences of people's decisions (both on themselves and others). Finally, I took the opportunity to leverage a strong, credible third party. As you know, the age-long principle of 'parents don't know anything' is still in play with your kids. So I used what I believe to be the most trusted and common-sense voice on the subject to speak to them – Dave Ramsey and his *Financial Peace University* program.

My sons are like the audience of an interactive play. Maybe you have participated in a dinner or play where the audience is an active participant in the story, and yet you know at the same time you're really also not responsible for the outcome, the actors are. My sons have been unwilling participants from the audience; they have been drawn in and get to be part of the play because they are in my family, but they are not responsible for the outcome, I am. Nevertheless, they get a unique experience that will be memorable.

PERSONAL ASSESSMENT - SPOKE #6: MONEY

1. Take an inventory of where you are personally.
    - Home Run – Why? What evidence is there?
    - Base Hit – Why? What evidence is there?
    - Strike Out – Why? What evidence is there?

2. What do you have to teach your son, either from doing it well or doing it wrong?
    - Where have you been successful, and what can you teach your son?
    - Where have you missed it, and what can you teach your son about it (what have you learned)?

3. What, if any, personal adjustments do you need to make to model well for your son?
    - As you assess your life currently against this spoke, Money, what needs to change in your life in order for there to be integrity with yourself and your son as you teach him to live well in this spoke?

4. What resources do you need to equip your son in this area that either reinforce your success, or may augment where you may be lacking personally?
    - Search out resources and teaching tools; books, classes, videos, seminars, mentors, etc., that either help illustrate and support your strength here, or augment your weakness and create a strength in both you and your son.

Tip: This is one of the really glaring areas of our lives, because it is usually right out there for everyone to see, including our sons. Most men have much to learn in this area, along with their sons. Don't hide your failures, but rather expose them, talk through them, and let them teach your son; after all, he is living with your strength or weakness in this area. Dave Ramsey, with his book Financial Peace, *is an incredible resource. He runs classes all over the United States for this program. I strongly encourage you and your son to get registered to go through it. I would also suggest that you seek out and find ordinary men who have been successful with finances, talk with them, and ask them what they did. I have found it most useful to seek out older men, those in their 60s, 70s, and 80s, primarily because these men know how to do it well. Most of them did it, not off from "get rich quick" schemes, or short cuts. They achieved financial success through self-discipline, hard work, a good work ethic, integrity, etc. Those are the things that create enduring financial freedom and peace. What you want to teach your boys here is not how to get wealthy, but how to have financial peace, and the principles that set you free.*

7th SPOKE: WORK
A LOST ETHIC

I'm a great believer in luck, and I find the harder I work the more I have of it.

–Thomas Jefferson

DO I HAVE TO?

This is the battle of the ages, or so it seems to us, the children of the Baby Boomer generation. As I talk to men of my age and generation, there is a common frustration expressed: the lack oftentimes of a strong, healthy work ethic in young men today. I see it all around me, and I even see it at times in my own sons. That is not a knock against my sons; in reality, we are all, generally speaking, lazy. We don't want to work; most of us work because we have to work. Some of us work because we want to, but for most of us, our default mode really is to do as little as possible.

If we are fortunate enough to find something that we love to do, that we are passionate about being involved in, then there is a different motivation to work. But in reality, it doesn't seem so much like work because of the fulfillment we find in it. Even these people will find this issue with work a problem when they are engaged in other endeavors that are not as exhilarating or fulfilling.

THE FALLACY OF THE SHORT CUT

The reason I have included this chapter is because I see a disturbing trend developing over the last couple of decades. If you are my age or older, you'll see it. If you are much younger than me, say early thirties or younger, you may miss it altogether because you are immersed in it; you were brought up in it. What is it? It's the short cut, the quick fix, the easiest route, and, a "least amount of effort required;" mentality. I know this is going to sound like I am bashing on everything that seems good and fun to us today, but I believe it is a direct reflection of the deterioration of our culture, and the diminished respect for traditional values. There seems to be a correlation between a deteriorating work ethic and the advent and escalation of technology; it seems we risk losing the all-powerful ethic of working hard. I am not necessarily suggesting there is a direct correlation, or cause and effect relationship, between technology and working hard. It's just an appropriate timeline. Similarly, you may have also noticed a rise in the "quick-fix" books, or the "quick-money" books. You may have also noticed the advent of some very creative financial instruments in the market, designed to create maximum return in minimum time, with minimal effort.

I remember the first time I heard and then read, "work smarter, not harder." I loved it; it seemed to make sense to me. It was exactly what this 30-something wanted to hear; I didn't have to work hard, I wanted to play. That's what I heard – I don't have to work hard! Do you realize that, if you were to take our base nature as a human and remove any motivation (food, sex, shelter, etc.), we would be amoeba-like blobs? Now I'm having a little fun with this, but seriously, who has not often experienced the moments when you have to make yourself get up and do what has to be done, and it was a great mental battle? We have nearly completely abandoned the idea of hard work as something to value and of which to be proud. It used to be a dearly held value, and a proud identifying characteristic for a man. It used to be a badge of honor to be known as a "hard worker." Not so much anymore. As a business consultant to large corporations who are hiring young people, you realize pretty quickly, as you spend time with these executives, how difficult it is to find workers with a good work ethic. Corporations and business owners are longing for hard workers, and when they find these workers, they are like gold to the employer.

THE GREAT PAMPERING

I believe part of the cause of this problem lies in the same thing that seems to be at the root of most of the other undesirable things we see developing in our young men: a lack of teaching them to be responsible and accountable. We do for them what they ought to do for themselves, when we should be intentionally putting them in positions to learn and grow through experience. We do this in both the little things and the big things, and in each case, we actually weaken them. We make them comfortable, because it's easier for us than taking the time to teach them valuable lessons, such as no work, no food! No work, no money! No work, no prom! No work, no movie! No work, no cell phone! No work, no...(fill in the blank)! We hand nearly everything over to them. They don't make any connection in their real world about work and privilege, about work and gain, or about work and living.

As I mentioned earlier, all this is easier to appreciate if you, like me, grew up in a time when it was normal to be out working at 14 or 15, and paying for some things yourself if you wanted them. Our society wasn't as affluent then. If you go back even further, dare I say to the "Greatest Generation," you saw something even more dramatic: whole families had to work simply just to eat. If you didn't work, you didn't live! Not an exaggeration. That generation knew something about work that we don't even remotely understand today, something that we have personally and directly benefited from. That generation knew how to work hard, and they built a great industrial nation. They also knew something that we may have lost sight of today: working hard and working smart are not mutually exclusive; they are synergistically linked. You must have both, as enduring success is not an "either-or proposition," it's "and both."

We have gotten so used to pampering our boys that when a common sense conversation comes up about working, we dads can sometimes be thought of as sweatshop owners. When I was 15 and 16, I was fishing in Alaska in the summers, and before that I was working at a restaurant far from my home. When I turned 16 and I was able to drive, I got other jobs closer to home and was working continually. I had to work if I wanted anything. A good work ethic is not the responsibility of a boss to instill, and it doesn't require a job outside of the home to teach it. It helps a man's formation to understand that there is a balance between work and play. Teaching a good work ethic can, and should, be done by the father at home, by example. It can be learned, as well, in athletics, and this is often a benefit we see from participating in sports. However, all too often we see it compartmentalized in sports and not taught nor required as a larger principle and virtue for all of life.

I see many younger married couples today whose husbands won't work. It's not that he can't work, but he won't work. He will draw unemployment instead of working, because he can make more money that way. I see men who decide that a certain type of work is beneath them, undignified in some way, so they won't work, as if taking care of your family, at any cost to yourself by working, does not in itself bestow dignity. I see young men who have no clue about the value of "hard work" as they enter the real world. They want to punch in and punch out as quickly as possible, and do only what is expected of them and no more. Why is this? Well, I believe that, as I mentioned before, this is our natural default mode. If our boys are not trained better, if they are not taught from an early age the natural consequences of laziness versus a good work ethic, if it is not modeled for them, they will revert to their default mode.

NO ESCAPING THE TRUTH

King Solomon, the author of several books in the Bible including Proverbs, in all his wisdom tried to teach his son (and us) this principle. On multiple occasions in Proverbs alone, he directly warns us about being lazy. In Proverbs, chapter 6, verses 10 and 11, and again in Proverbs, chapter 14, verses 33 and 34, he says, "*A little extra sleep, a little more slumber, a little folding of the hands to rest – then poverty will pounce on you like a bandit; scarcity will attack you like an armed robber."* He gave the exact same set of instructions twice. I think it is important, and all I have to do is look at my own life to know it's true. Simultaneously, he also taught us the benefit of work in Proverbs, chapter 12, verse 14, *hard work brings rewards*, and in verse 24, *Work hard and become a leader; be lazy and become a slave.* Finally, in the Book of Ecclesiastes, Solomon says in chapter 10, verse 15, *Fools are so exhausted by a little work that they can't even find their way home.* He draws a direct correlation to a lazy person and a fool. There is much more on this subject in both the Old and New Testaments of the Bible. A side note here: I also believe that vision and goals have a lot to do with a young man's motivation level. That is addressed in Chapter 7, Direction: Vision, Values and Goals.

IT'S AN HONOR THING

Men, if you have a son, and if you're reading this book you probably do, or you at least care about someone who does, then it is imperative that we embrace a good work ethic as an ethos in our sons' lives. This, once again, will call you to be countercultural. Your sons may not like it much, that's for sure. Your wife may not understand you as you begin to instill the habits and disciplines of a good work ethic in your sons.   Privileges come with proper handling of responsibilities; if your son is not going to have a good work ethic at home, then maybe he should not experience the privileges and benefits, i.e., have a phone, or dinner, or a bed, or be allowed to borrow the car, and so on.

So what is a good work ethic? People may define it differently, but here is something for you to consider:

You give your best; you give more than is expected; you do more than is asked; you do what needs to be done without asking; you strive for excellence at the task before you, whether you like it or not, because you take pride in a job well done; you arrive early, and you stay late when necessary; you do what can be done now, rather than putting it off until tomorrow; you take pride in the approval of those whose opinions matter; you take gratification from a job well done.

A good work ethic is a noble and virtuous thing, and something to take personal pride in all by itself, regardless of the thing at which you are laboring. We must understand this and get this into our sons' heads and hearts. It doesn't matter if they enjoy the task as much as the pride they take in how they perform it. Something that has crept into our cultural conversation is the idea of fulfilling work or purposeful work. I agree that it is more desirable to work at something that is enjoyable and personally fulfilling. Unfortunately, though, men are using this as an excuse not to work, or at least not to give their best. Work, that is, providing for your family, not being a drag on others, and giving your best because it is right, is purposeful and rewarding and virtuous all by itself. When he works, a man can, and should, take a certain sense of pride and purpose in that fact alone.

RESISTANCE IS NOT FUTILE

Because of my circumstances, I learned to work hard. I learned early that if I wanted something, I was going to have to work for it. I believe that, although it wasn't fun, it was immensely good for me. This was not an intentional process of teaching by my dad, but I, nevertheless, learned to work, and work hard. However, I was challenged as a father when things were going well financially. I found myself doing things for my sons that were unintentionally unprofitable for them, providing things for them without them understanding the correlation between earning and having, between sacrifice and reward. I would then find myself getting frustrated with my boys because they weren't working hard.

If you are a father, you know what I mean. Just try to get them to do some yard work, and have it done well. I would get frustrated with them, maybe even rant at them for not working hard. What I should have been doing, rather than ranting and raving, was simply and calmly, withhold privileges, creating natural consequences for their choice not to have a good work ethic. The things they took for granted, being my sons, could, in reality, be great tools in helping them associate a good work ethic with having privileges. I finally got it, although a little late. I have found it is a powerful and effective tool with them. They are getting it. We still will deal with the laziness issue from time to time, but much less than before. They are good sons, learning good lessons, and making their father proud.

I was caught in the cultural, pitiful "my kids should have it better than me" trap. I don't know where this attitude came from, but it may have done more to damage our young men than any other single prevailing attitude. Who says our kids should have it better than us? Where did this attitude come from? What exactly do we mean by that statement: more stuff, more money, an easier life, less stress? Although I believe some fathers are well-intentioned, they do not really understanding the consequences of this attitude as it relates to our young men and the subsequent attitudes they develop. If by that statement we mean something synonymous with "easier" or "less demanding" or "more privilege" than we had growing up, then we do this to their detriment, and to the detriment of our society.

I am teaching a strong work ethic to my sons. It's not fun for them or for me at times, but it's worth every moment of discomfort now in order to see them excel as men, husbands, and fathers in the future. The fruit of my labor may be like some of the other "spokes" in this book; it will be in the future. I may not be seeing the full expression of this key in them right now, but I believe I will. I hope and trust they will remember what they have learned and seen demonstrated. I hope and trust they will apply it in their lives and be good men with a strong work ethic that will make me, their mother, and their wives and kids proud.

You may find that you have to go back a ways to find that noble quality of a good work ethic. It's not often readily present today. It's out there, although you have to look a little harder to find it. When you do, you must recognize and applaud it before your sons. You must lead by example, as well, just as with any other principle in this book. You may see other men's sons who appear to "get it" better than your sons. Do not despair, and do not compare. Your sons don't need to be manipulated by guilt or shame into this quality. Keep the expectation high, and be patient. Teach by allowing consequences to do the work they are designed to do. Set the example, then loudly and proudly acknowledge their success.

PERSONAL ASSESSMENT - SPOKE #7: WORK

1. Take an inventory of where you are personally.
   - Home Run – Why? What evidence is there?
   - Base Hit – Why? What evidence is there?
   - Strike Out – Why? What evidence is there?

2. What do you have to teach your son, either from doing it well or doing it wrong?

- Where have you been successful, and what can you teach your son?
- Where have you missed it, and what can you teach your son about it (what have you learned)?

3. What, if any, personal adjustments do you need to make to model well for your son?
   - As you assess your life currently against this spoke, Work, what needs to change in order for there to be integrity with yourself and your son as you teach him to live well in this spoke?

4. What resources do you need to equip your son in this area that either reinforce your success, or may augment where you may be lacking personally?
   - Search out resources and teaching tools: books, classes, videos, seminars, mentors, etc. that either help illustrate and support your strength here, or augment your weakness and create a strength in both you and your son.

Tip: This one may be tough for which to find good examples. The work ethic has so declined in our culture that it's not easy to find good examples. But they are out there. Use your life as an example if you are a hard worker, but augment it with other examples. You may have even been personally challenged by this chapter. Remember, these things are caught and taught, so immediately ask yourself how you can personally model a classic, excellent work ethic for your son. Do you sleep-in in the mornings when you could be up and cleaning your garage, reading your Bible, or taking care of your yard, when all these things are in some kind of disarray? Do you roll out of the house at the last minute and barely get to work on time? Do you come home and complain about your work in your son's hearing? Have you gotten comfortable with an element of laziness in your life? Do you sit around and watch television when the lawn needs to be mowed, the car needs to be washed, or your wife needs help with the dishes? You will also find your very best models for this spoke of work ethic in older men, similar to the other areas of this book. You will also find excellent examples with entrepreneurs. Seek them out, sit with them, and listen and learn from them.

THIRTEEN

8th SPOKE: THE "STRETCH"
FINDING THEIR LIMITS

When we argue for our limitations, we get to keep them.

– Evelyn Waugh

WHAT MAKES US MEN

It is not possible to look backward into the history and purpose of the rite of passage and not be inspired, as a man, by the physical and psychological challenges young men had to face. It brings to your mind words and ideals such as courage, honor, valor, and strength. I will readily admit that these things might create more of a stir in me than in other men, but I do believe that I represent the vast majority of men. It is why I was intentional with some of the movies and characters I mentioned earlier in this book. They inspire us, as men, and stir up in us something that is innate in us: the desire to be heroic, courageous, to face a challenge, and be victorious. Suppressing this urge is part of the problem we have today with men. We are told that it's old-fashioned, unnecessary, harmful, or chauvinistic. However, nothing is farther from the truth, when properly channeled. My personal belief is that, as men, we need to embrace that part of our nature.

John Eldredge's groundbreaking book *Wild at Heart*[1], and the follow-up book *The Way of the Wild Heart*[2], were very significant in my life. *Wild at Heart* created an awakening in me about real masculinity, how it has been suppressed in our culture, and how that has left a deeply unmet need in men today. *The Way of the Wild Heart* was helpful to inspire me in the development of my sons. I recommend you read both of these books. John articulates the heart of a man, what is at the core of every man as he is designed by God, and the unshakable need to express that design. A man is not truly fulfilled in his soul without this authentic expression of his masculinity. This quest for testing our limits, our "stretch," is not about risk-taking, but it is most often expressed and realized this way.

DRAW IT OUT OF THEM

Part of that discovery is finding our limits, pushing our physical and psychological boundaries, getting to the edge of ourselves, and finding out there is more to us than we thought. We do not know what we are capable of until we are tested. And we are often surprised when we discover we are able to do more than we thought, that there is more strength, stamina, will, and drive in us than we knew. It is also not normal for us to do this to ourselves; it usually takes a catalyst in our lives to bring us to these places. For an athlete, it may be a coach. For a climber, it's a guide and fellow climbers. For a soldier, it's a drill instructor or combat. For a firefighter or policeman, it's a crisis like 9/11.

As a father, I felt it was my responsibility to be the catalyst for my boys, to create an event that stretched them to their limits of endurance and strength. I believe it is my responsibility to help them discover something significant about themselves as men, how to get to the edge, and then go a little further because you have to. I was also looking forward to the lessons they would learn about discipline, comfort zones, hard work, preparation, and the like.

OUR STRETCH

Because I enjoy hiking in the Cascade Mountains in Washington, I decided that the stretch for my boys would be to climb Mt. Adams, with a summit of 12,300 feet. Mt. Adams sees a lot of people climb the summit each year, because it has a non-technical approach. It is just physically daunting. I wanted my boys to experience standing on top of a mountain peak, looking out across the hemisphere, with me standing next to them. I knew this was going to be tough on them, extracting something from them that had never been mined before. The training was going to be tough all by itself for them, building their endurance and stamina. To summit would be a personal challenge for them, one they would never forget. And for us to do it together was a bonding experience I would treasure forever. I realized that they might not fully appreciate the experience in its fullest measure until later, maybe even when they are adults and have boys of their own. But I did know it would be a defining moment for them, for us as father and sons, and a marker for the rest of their lives.

My boys are very different: personality, physically, everything; what comes easily for one is quite demanding for the other. I knew this trip would test both of them, and bring out their strengths and weaknesses. My younger son, Brendan, is more athletic and agile, much smaller and nimbler. My older son, Devan, is less athletic, but very thoughtful, pragmatic, self-aware, and contemplative. Devan is conservative; Brendan is a risk-taker. I knew this was going to be a classic tortoise and hare type of competition between the two of them, and it was fun and interesting to watch how each of them responded to the challenges, and there were plenty.

DEVAN – THE TEST IS IN THE JOURNEY

We began running, and we conducted some smaller hikes locally to build endurance. Brendan would run up the hillside or little mountain with me. Devan would be methodical and pace himself. Brendan would tease and test; Devan would ignore him and keep moving. This part of the training was much easier for Brendan than Devan. I was extraordinarily proud of Devan, though; it was more demanding on him physically than any of the three of us, and he never gave up! I was hard on him during this phase, because I knew he could do more than he thought, and I wanted him to discover what he was made of. We climbed a steep, little hill, famous in our area, called Mt. Peak (1,800 feet). It was our litmus test to show how far we had come in our conditioning. We climbed Mt. Si (4,100 feet), we climbed Granite Mountain (5,600 feet), and other local places in preparation for Mt. Adams. The boys hated me for a season in their lives as I dragged them out in the morning and up these mountains at uncomfortable paces.

It was on one of these climbs where Devan had his moment of truth. It was Mt. Si. He had just come from a three-day conference at our church where he had been serving. He had long days, little sleep on hard floors, and hadn't eaten well. He came home early on a Friday morning, and slept almost the whole day. We got up on Saturday morning early and headed for Mt. Si. I was really pushing the boys to reach a goal of hitting the top in two hours or less. I didn't realize it at the time, but Devan was really dehydrated and had some level of exhaustion lingering from the previous three days. As we got about halfway to the top, I noticed Devan beginning to slow down. He began to complain of being tired and not feeling well. I pushed him.

When we got to about three-quarters of the way to the top he was really not doing great; he was sweating profusely, a little nauseous, but we were so close to the top. When we got within a couple hundred feet of the top, he hit the wall. I could see he was really not doing well, getting lethargic, and not hydrating properly. I encouraged him to finish, as we only had a couple hundred feet to go. Devan, not wanting to disappoint me said, "Okay, let's finish." As I recount this experience now, I have a lot of emotion working up in me, as my gentle giant of a son appeased his father and pushed on. Just before we got to the top, he stopped, turned to me, and said, "Dad, I don't know if I can make it," and then began to fall backwards. I grabbed him, propped him up, and told him we couldn't stop there. We were in the middle of a rocky climbing area, and there was no place to rest. We pushed that last few feet to the top, and there, on top of Mt. Si, my son Devan lost consciousness and fell into my arms.

It was the most frightening moment of my life. I called 911, and as they were sending a rescue team, I called my friends to have them begin to pray for Devan. I began to pray and hold my son. There was nothing I could do. Devan was unconscious for nearly 45 minutes. He awoke just before the search and rescue team arrived. They took his vitals, assessed him, and determined that it was a combination of dehydration and extreme exhaustion. We walked him out about a mile to an old logging road, where the rescue team put Devan and I in one truck, and the rest of the guys in other trucks, and took us all down. He spent the next two days resting, rehydrating, and getting his strength back.

That's not the end of the story, however, for Devan and Mt. Si. The following week, seven days later, we went back to Mt. Si to climb it again. In the days that preceded us going back, I talked to Devan about either giving up at this point, or pushing forward through this experience. We talked about how this experience could be defining for him, either way. He chose to go back to Mt. Si. A week to the day that Mt. Si had gotten the best of Devan, Devan got the best of Mt. Si. He stood on the very spot where, a week earlier, he had been lying on his back, unconscious. And he did it in two hours! Devan learned something about himself through that experience, and there was a real moment of pride and achievement in him as he stood victorious on Mt. Si.

BRENDAN – THE TEST IS IN THE JOURNEY

Brendan's test came on the actual climb on Mt. Adams. He did well in the pre-training and hiking and climbing, but on this day, with his full pack on his little frame, that was a different story. He had been a little cocky up to that point in our training, but when he put on the pack that was one-third his body weight, a little air was let out of his balloon, so to speak. Brendan was a pretty small boy; he was under both height and weight for his age, and my boy had sticks for legs. I knew he could climb like a mountain goat, but I also knew some weight was really going to slow him down. When we set off from the Cold Springs Camp Grounds, he was all energy, and a little too prideful, as he ignored my encouragement to pace himself and slow down, but he didn't want to listen. By the time we got about 1/3 of the way to the overnight camping spot, Lunch Counter, he was really starting to struggle. He was no longer out front; he was in the back, and his swagger was gone.

I began to pace with him and let the others get ahead. I encouraged him, but he was clearly running out of gas. I continued to push him right up until I didn't think he could do much more, and then we stopped. I looked at my little man; he was trying so hard, but he was also coming face to face, for the first time for him, with discovering his limits. I finally told him to take off his pack and set it down. He did, thinking we were going to rest a little, and then get going again. But after a few minutes of rest, when I knew no one else could see us, I picked up my pack and slung it over one shoulder, and grabbed his pack and slung it over my other shoulder. I said, "Let's go, son," and he was furious with me. He was not going to have any of that for a moment. He looked me in the eye, all five feet and 80 pounds of him, and said, "Dad, no one else is going to carry my pack." I tried to reason with him for a bit, but I was enormously proud that the more I insisted, the more he resisted. Finally, I relented, put his pack on his back, and Brendan methodically, in pain at times and thoroughly exhausted, continued on to Lunch Counter. We got there a little later than the rest, but the Brendan that arrived at Lunch Counter was a little different than the Brendan that left Cold Springs Camp Grounds. He had the opportunity to quit on himself, having come to what he thought was his physical limits. Like Devan and Mt. Si, Brendan chose that day not to quit, but to forge on.

THE POINT OF IT ALL

There is something in every man that has to come to that place where he is faced with these kinds of moments and decides to forge on. It can look different for different men, and for their sons. But I do believe these stretch moments, where your will and your physical and mental strength are tested, are essential for the formation of every son and man. We all have different tolerances for risk and danger. This isn't about a dangerous outing where someone's life is at peril as you're hanging off a cliff face or something like that. Sometimes that can be more about bravado and thrill-chasing. This is an intentional process of discovery for your son. This experience with my boys is about much more than climbing Mt. Adams. One day, they will face a situation or situations in life, and it will demand more of them than they think they have. They will have their Mt. Adams experience and their father to remind them, to encourage them, and to motivate them to stay in the battle, knowing they can rise to the challenge, whatever it may be. No quitting! This does something in the heart and soul of a man that I cannot fully put into words. But I believe that until he has this kind of experience, he is not fully developed.

We all reached the summit of Mt. Adams the next day. It wasn't easy; that day was just as challenging for Devan as Mt. Si was, and it was just as challenging for Brendan as the previous day up to Lunch Counter had been. But we made it together! I have a picture of the group standing on top of the mountain that I will cherish forever, and it will be a marker for my boys for the rest of their lives. For my sons and me, this rounded out the rite of passage, and brought it to a full experience. It came late for Devan in his experience, and earlier for Brendan, but it came. They had the experience, and they had it together, which, if you have more than one son, is pretty cool.

So, father, what will your son's "stretch" be? There are lots of things a man can do with his son to have this experience. It could be through sports, although I would encourage you to make it more intimate with you. It could be a wilderness type of expedition; there are lots of opportunities for guided experiences, or get equipped and do it on your own. Enjoyment is not the primary goal for your sons; although I would encourage you to make it fun, at least at points. My boys were not enthusiastic about climbing Mt. Adams. And they didn't fall in love with this type of hiking as a result. But I knew what they needed, I knew a way to create it, and I made a point of making it fun and memorable as often as possible. Make it significant, and make it grand, because it will be a bonding experience on which you will never be able to put a price. Think outside of the box: what does your part of the country offer? I have mountains; what do you have? Create the "stretch!"

PERSONAL ASSESSMENT - SPOKE #8: THE STRETCH

1. Take an inventory of where you are personally.
   - Home Run – Why? What evidence is there?
   - Base Hit – Why? What evidence is there?
   - Strike Out – Why? What evidence is there?

2. What do you have to teach your son, either from doing it well or doing it wrong?
   - Where have you been successful, and what can you teach your son?
   - Where have you missed it, and what can you teach your

son about it (what have you learned)?

3. What, if any, personal adjustments do you need to make to model well for your son?
    *   As you assess your life currently against this spoke, The Stretch, what needs to change in order for there to be integrity with yourself and your son, as you teach him to live well in this spoke?

4. What resources do you need to equip your son in this area that either reinforce your success, or may augment where you may be lacking personally?
    *   Search out resources and teaching tools: books, classes, videos, seminars, mentors, etc that either help illustrate and support your strength here, or augment your weakness and create a strength in both you and your son.

Tip: You may lean in one of two directions here: Intense or passive. Too intense, and you can intimidate your sons and cause them to feel inferior. Too passive, and you can cause your boys never to "go for it." You also must know your own sons personality well. My two boys could not be more different, as I have noted. This is not about making them like you, but helping them, based on their personality, understand what they CAN do. Seek out activities with other men who have a variety of ranges when it comes to risk-taking; this will help your boys find their place, and help you stay in balance. Make friends with men that have experiences you don't have, who are involved in activities you would like to discover, and have them take you and your sons. Be creative, and maybe this will even stretch you, as well.

FOURTEEN

PREPARING YOUR WIFE
THE FORGOTTEN CHAPTER

People are generally down on what they are not up on.

– Unknown

THE LAUNCH SEQUENCE

A funny thing happened on the way to helping my boys become men…I didn't think about my wife! I thought about her in one sense by talking to her about what I was doing, the goal for the rite of passage, getting her input, and those sorts of things. She was enthusiastic and supportive. So far, so good. But I did not think about her personally, about being prepared emotionally for the reality of what was to come. There is a sequence to follow!

Part of the rite of passage is preparing your young man to leave the home and strike out on his own. It's not good for a boy to live with his mom and dad after a certain point. It actually becomes very unproductive and enabling, and it hurts him. The reality is that most people don't take responsibility until it is thrust upon them. Taking on responsibility often has the potential to be uncomfortable, and people will resist. So part of this process over the last several years has been the consistent messaging to my boys that when they are 18 and out of high school, they are out of the house.

For me, there are some exceptions to that hard and fast rule. If they are in college full time and working, among other things, they can stay at home. If they have a plan for exiting the house, and are working and saving money with very specific goals, then the matter is open for conversation. But when they are done with school, they don't just get to hang out at home and work at McDonald's, heading nowhere. It's not my intention to deride McDonald's. My point is about the son who is flipping burgers and has no vision beyond that moment. Some people go on to develop a great career in that industry. The question for your son would be, "Why am I there"? And rent isn't an issue. I am not interested in being a landlord to my kids, which, in my experience in working with others, creates interesting dynamics in the relationship. If my son stays here under acceptable circumstances, he will pay his expenses, but we will not have a landlord tenant relationship.

INTERRUPTION IN THE SEQUENCE

I have been preparing my sons for this moment for years. And three years ago, my wife heard the conversations and it was no big deal. However, when the moment was drawing ever-so-close as my oldest son was nearing graduation, the emotions were running high, and the tension was getting thicker. My wife is a wonderful mother, protective of her kids, who cares for and loves them intensely. What I see as a responsible action by moving my son into taking responsible action, she sees as frightening and exposing her son to all sorts of untold danger and peril. I also began to realize how much of her identity was wrapped up in being their mom. I also realized how important it was that we have the same definition for the ultimate purpose of parenting.

It occurred to me that, while this process is excellent in its intention, it would have been much better to sit down long ago and talk about the specifics of how this would roll out. She wouldn't have had issues so much with the principles, but the particulars were snags. I should have included my wife in the long-term end goal of our sons leaving home at 18, and allowed her input and participation to get buy-in and perspective. The old adage I have used for years immediately came into play: "people are down on what they are not up on." And this certainly had come true with my dear wife. She didn't disagree with the principles, but when the moment was actually closing in, the principles didn't matter as much any more. She was struggling with her role change as her son's life transitioned from boy to man. So we've had a little fun, my son and I, teasing her about him moving out. It hasn't been so funny to her, though. As that potential day drew closer, the emotions and tension got higher.

LOGIC DOES NOT ALWAYS RULE

It's easy for me to get an attitude about it all, and just simply say that I know better. The truth is that I have studied, read, researched, and interviewed those who have done this well, and those who have not. I am pretty confident, in fact, fully persuaded, that what I am doing is right and good. But this is not about reasoning or logic; this is about the emotional realities of a mom's child leaving, and her grappling with her new role. I am not deceived; I have had moments thinking about this day coming, and they have been a little emotionally challenging for me, as well, but I'm also exhilarated at watching my son leave the nest and fly on his own. I'm excited to see how all our time together and training coalesce.

Nevertheless, this is much more challenging for my wife. Men, preparing your wife is as important as preparing your son. If your son has reservations and anxiety and doubt about the future, she will have many more, and he will find someone to sympathize with in his mom. So you need to take the time early on to bring your wife into the process, clearly define and agree on what your roles as parents are, and how you will go about executing that responsibility. Once this is defined, you will have to remind her of this continually, and be patient and understanding as she navigates the emotions and realities. I did not do this well at times, but she knew I loved my boys, she knew I had prepared, and she knew she wanted to see her boys succeed as men. I know there are things my wife must cease doing for our sons that are simply convenient for them, but are part of her identity as a mother:

- Making his lunch
- Doing his laundry
- Waking him up in the morning for school/work
- Reminding him of things to do
- Doting over him when he doesn't feel well

The list goes on and on. And God bless the Mother, and I mean that very literally! But it will feel like a literal tearing of her flesh during part of this process, and you will have to peel her away from some of these activities, literally, at least I did. That is why it is so crucial to begin the conversation early. You must paint the picture for her, and give her a clear vision of where you are going and why you are going there with your son. Help her to understand that it is why you have children; you were given them for this very moment, to successfully release them and send them into the world to make a difference, and, if you're a Christian, to be "salt and light."

REINITIATE LAUNCH SEQUENCE

Most would agree that the responsibility of parents is to prepare their kids to be productive, participating, responsible, successful, contributing members of society. As parents, we are raising adults, preparing them for release to begin their own lives, families, careers, etc., and to find their own purpose in life. Most of us would generally agree with that definition. Once you and your wife have agreed on what your responsibility is to your children, to prepare them to successfully leave the nest, then you can have a conversation about what this looks like practically, keeping the purpose in mind. You have an opportunity to be like the incredible dynamic duo, the father and mother eagle, working together in unity toward the inevitable. You will have to come back continually to your purpose as parents. This will help your wife prepare to release her fledgling adult. Include her in the process all the way along, keeping her informed, and involving her. If your sons are young, say 4 or 5 years old, that is a great time to get a vision, and to begin to talk to your wife about your roles and responsibilities as parents to create men and prepare your sons for release.

It's important that you acknowledge and honor her feelings, and let her talk about them and not react to them, or take a defensive position in what you are doing. I didn't do such a great job in this area. I would often become resentful of what I perceived were my wife's efforts to hinder me in my goal. There were times of real conflict, because we just simply did not agree on certain things I was doing. Your wife needs to have a voice, and when she has been heard, remind her of your purpose as parents, and come back to a place of agreement. It's helpful, also, to remind her, occasionally, of all the stories of parents who have not done this well (your own may be one of them) and the havoc that is generated in those people's lives, as well as all the irresponsible, underdeveloped, and immature men out there who have never learned, nor were forced to take, responsibility. It will be helpful to remind her that you, together, are raising a young man who needs to be given independence and responsibility in order to become fully mature.

Men, the process will be challenging enough at times, so out of respect for your wife, and for the benefit of the success of the process and for the good of your son, prepare your wife. Start early and visit it often.

LEADING CAN BE LONELY

At the risk of sounding chauvinistic or dictatorial, you may have moments when you know you are doing the right thing and it needs to be done, and you may not have the willing participation of your wife or son. But you must do it anyway. There is a leadership principal that my friend and pastor, Roger Archer, teaches: You must be understanding, while being misunderstood, until they understand. Throughout this process, I had to be understanding with my wife and sons, while being misunderstood by them, until they understand. You may walk this path alone from time to time, but leaders often will have to do things that others are unwilling or unable to do. You will have moments where you will question your decisions, and some of them won't be right. Be humble and honest with your wife; arrogance and withholding produces ugly results. Remember, your two natures are very different, and it takes both of you to bring balance. Engage her in the process; she will bring immense value. You need her as your partner; she was created for this purpose.

Remember the story of the eagles in the introduction? It is a great illustration of how important her role is, and it's your responsibility to lead her into this understanding. I invite you to reread that story again as you close out this chapter. God did not make a mistake with husbands and wives, fathers and mothers. When we work together, our sons have a real chance.

FIFTEEN

DEVELOPING YOUR PLAN

He who fails to plan is planning to fail.

– Winston Churchill

PLANNING AND EXECUTION

There is a book that I enjoyed reading a number of years ago, and the title says it all, *The Knowing Doing Gap.*[1] There is a gap between what we know and what we do. The problem isn't that we don't know enough. In most cases, we have enough knowledge, we just don't apply it; there is a "doing" problem.

You have some new knowledge after reading this far into the book, or at a minimum, you have had some things you know confirmed or reinforced. When I counsel with couples about their marriage, or parents in regard to their kids, it isn't very often that there is some new and brilliant revelation. It's usually just affirming what they already know, have learned or heard, forgotten or ignored, and moving them to take action on existing knowledge.

Let's close the gap between what you know and what you do. Your boys, family legacy, and maybe the future of our society depend on it. There are a few steps to consider as you develop your personal rite of passage for your son. But it's not just a matter of a good plan. A mediocre plan executed is better than an excellent plan sitting on the table. You need a plan and you need execution.

FIRST, A FEW THINGS THAT MATTER

Timing matters. It matters when you start the rite of passage for your son, and it is based on his maturity. Every person matures differently, and you must know when your son is mature enough to: a) understand the concepts; b) retain the lessons you are teaching; c) pay attention to you; d) make real emotional and mental connections to the information; and e) apply the concepts. My sons were different. There are many things that affect the maturity of a person, from how they are hard wired, to birth order, to parenting, and my sons were no exception. I started my older son a little earlier than my second son. I just knew my boys, and they were different from each other. I celebrate each of them and their uniqueness, and I love that about them both. But I knew my second son wasn't ready to sit still for one hour every Friday at age 13. We had to wait a little longer.

Timeline matters. I believe, on average, it should take about 12 - 14 months to walk through your process. This may seem long, but it allows you to break up the process into bite-size nuggets. The most updated research about learning reveals that we learn best when we get a nugget that we can chew on, time to digest it, and then put it into practice. What we tend to do is feed our kids and others information with a fire hose and hope that the majority makes it in, or there is no intentionality at all, and hope is our only strategy. This is just inconsistent with all the research about the best learning methods. At the end of the day, we are more concerned about quality than quantity.

Environment matters. You want to make sure that it's as enjoyable as possible for your son. He will get bored easily, so make sure you create an environment that he will look forward to. Conducting your rite of passage in a location or setting that is unique and makes your son feel important is essential to success.

He will look forward to it, he will stay engaged in the process, and it will be memorable. This is why I set up our sessions once a week, for one hour at Starbucks. This achieves multiple goals. By meeting at Starbucks, it communicates that this is special and makes my sons feel valued. By keeping it to an hour, they stay engaged and don't get too bored. By doing it once a week, it gives us a week to chew on the things we discussed. I buy them a coffee of their choice, which also makes them feel important.

Fun matters. Remember, they are boys! I took this opportunity to teach my boys how to drive. They would drive to Starbucks on Friday morning, and then to school afterwards. It was a great bonding time, and a great motivator for getting them excited about Friday mornings. I interspersed our trips and dinners along the way to keep some anticipation and fun in the process, when it could otherwise get a little dry or monotonous.

Memory matters. During this process, you are building a memorial by creating a memory book. This book contains key items to memorialize the journey for your son: letters, photos, memorabilia from your trips, and so on.

DESIGNING YOUR SON'S RITE OF PASSAGE

You need to design and calendar the overall process. How do you launch the rite of passage, how do you make it memorable, how do you create an expectation, what special events do you plan to create a bond with your son, and finally, how does the process culminate to create a landmark event in his life? For my boys and me, these were the four components:

> **Inaugural dinner:** At this dinner, I brought together three men that I highly respect. These men optimize the qualities and characteristics that I want my boys to see and emulate. These are

men that have all been on both sides of life, like me, and found their way, and they have something to say worth listening to about being a quality man.

This dinner took place at a nice restaurant of my son's choosing. I opened the dinner with prayer, explained why we were gathered, and why this process is important. I didn't make a long-winded speech. I was specific. I told a story from my life to illustrate, and then moved on. I had each of the men write a letter to my son in advance, and I told them it would be part of a "memory book" we would be putting together, so make it nice. I had each man read his letter to my son, and asked him to share personally from his life. The goal was for each man to impart wisdom to my son and speak affirming words over his life in regard to his potential as a man of quality. When we were done, we all placed our hands on my son, and we each took a moment to pray over him. We ate a great meal and had a good time during this process. I took pictures of the event that were placed into his memory book.

The Journey: I sat down and calendared out 18 months, that is, 72 Fridays. You'll lose a couple of Fridays because of your trips. A few Fridays will slip away because of vacations and such; life happens. So I typically end up with about 62 Fridays. This is not cast in stone; it could be more or less depending on you and your son. I divide the 8 principles over those 62 Fridays. For example, I spend:

- Weeks 1-10: Faith and the book *A Case for Christ* (build the hub)
- Weeks 11-22: Foundation building in the book of *Proverbs*
- Weeks 23-28: Values, vision and goals (2 weeks each)
- Weeks 29-32: Chivalry & proper attitudes towards women

- Weeks 33-44: Sexual integrity
- Weeks 45-56: Relationships and dealing with people
- Weeks 57-60: Finances and stewardship
- 2 weeks wrapping up, summarizing, and preparing for graduation

These are broken down in greater detail in the father's planner, a supplement to the rite of passage, and the accompanying journal for your son.

The issues of character and integrity, how to treat a woman, and work ethic, the areas that don't have a specific teaching book, are easily talked about as you are going through Proverbs and other material, although you may have, or know of, great books to use with your sons. You will find lots of opportunities to cover each of these areas. You may even choose to use this book as a resource in some of these areas.

At the end of each spoke, I require my son to write a one-page synopsis of what he has learned and how he will live as a result of his learning. I am looking for both principles and specifics. What I am looking for is a document that, if he read it aloud to some people, they would get it. And that is exactly what he will do; at his graduation ceremony, he will read these eight pages. It's how I know he got it, and they will go into his memory book.

Mid-term trips: We took two mid-term trips; these trips marked midway points and broke up the process. This also created anticipation. We took a trip a few months into it, and another a just before the end.

The mid-term trip we took depended on the individual boy's interest. It was about them, not me. We took a few days and got away, just the two of us. For my older son who enjoys golf, we took a golfing trip. For my younger son, who enjoys skating and snowboarding, we took a winter ski trip. These trips were real highpoints in their rite of passage. We did real guy things that were big to them. At this time, I also tried to do things that are a little on the fringe, but create lasting memories. On these trips, I allowed the boys to drive, which helped solidify this as the event of a lifetime.

Graduation ceremony: This was an elaborate and special event, which included important people in their life, to recognize their achievement and acknowledge their transition from a boy to a man.

This is the pinnacle of the process, the high point. I did the most planning and preparation at this point. I invited the people that would endure in the boy's life: close friends, relatives who shared our values, grandparents, and so on. I also invited people who may have watched our son grow up. I used this opportunity to expose other dads with young boys to this concept of a rite of passage. This dinner included:

- A recap of our process by me (my reflections of this journey with my son).
- My son sharing his personal reflections and high points, what he learned, and what he will take away (usually reading his summary sheets and ad-libbing).
- A few people who shared their observations of the change in my son over this time (they were invited to speak prior to the event, but at the event it is spontaneous and voluntary).
- A covenant to solidify his commitment to sexual integrity. This is a declared commitment by him, made to all present (a sample of this is provided in the father's planner).
- I speak a blessing over his life. This is a pattern established

in the Bible, and it is an opportunity to declare affirmatively and authoritatively the promises and hopes and beliefs for your son's future (a sample is provided in the father's planner).

- The presentation of a sword with scripture from the Bible engraved on it, one that was appropriate for his personality (I choose a sword, because of it's symbolism: courage, strength, battling, honor, etc.).

POST RITE OF PASSAGE

Now the real challenges and opportunities present themselves. Your son has now transitioned into manhood. It's time to treat him differently. Ideally, your son is very close to 16, and this gives him two years to practice under your care and covering so he is ready to launch at 18. I used the analogy of an astronaut with my boys. They just don't go from Navy pilot on a flight deck to Astronaut in space. They have very important phases to prepare them to be successful. They go through rigorous training (a rite of passage), then spend time practicing in a simulator where they can make mistakes and learn without killing themselves or others (ages 16–18, following the rite of passage), and finally, they are launched into their mission (leaving home).

Your relationship with your son changes with each phase. You no longer treat him as a child; you now become his coach and consultant (to borrow a term from my pastor). You allow him to learn, crash and burn, you pick him up, and you talk to him more as an equal and not so much as a child. This is where he begins to take on serious, personal accountability for his life. And this is where you can begin to see the friction between you and your wife develop as she may attempt to rescue him from his decisions and consequences, or at a minimum, deflect some of the impact.

This can range from getting himself up in the morning and ready for school, to getting a job and working, to paying his own way for stuff, to the way he treats his family and women as he begins dating, and so on. It includes allowing him to stretch his wings and learn some lessons, rather than just telling him. Experience is an excellent teacher, and natural consequences are the best tutor. The way I stated it with my boys was like this: Take some chances and learn your lessons while you're under my roof, my care, and my covering, so that you don't make major mistakes when you are out on your own.

In a conversation with my older son, Devan, we talked about the whole astronaut and shuttle analogy. They don't just jump into the cockpit of the shuttle and take off. The stakes are way too high. They spend time practicing, learning, and making mistakes in the safety of a simulator. This doesn't guarantee that they don't make a mistake, but it does ensure that, a) it's much less likely they will, and b) if they do, they know how to recover. That's what the time in between the graduation ceremony and when they turn 18 and leave the house is all about: simulation is preparation. It was an analogy they could understand, and it created an atmosphere that allowed freedom, risk, error, recovery, and success.

Both of my sons are living at home. Devan has finished high school, he just got his Associates of Arts degree from a local community college, and he is transferring to a local four year college. He is still at home because he is going to college full time, working nearly full time, and paying his way. He is adhering to our values, being responsible, and saving money. He has goals and a plan. Brendan is finishing up high school. He is still in the simulator stage, and he's learning much about life and himself. In the years that have followed my sons' rites of passage, we have continued to spend time together, having fun and getting away on little adventures, reading together, sitting down and talking through options, missteps, and successes, and I use those opportunities regularly to bring them back to the things they learned in their rite of passage. I intentionally look for people and opportunities to expose them to for great modeling for their lives.

For example, every Saturday morning the three of us get together at Starbucks (I buy), and we are going through the book *Mere Christianity* by C.S. Lewis. Another example, I had a young man by my house the other day for a painting estimate. He is 23, has his Bachelor's degree, he is running his own business and doing well, with big goals for the future. As he was giving me his estimate, he had a little "bio" in his packet. I found it very intriguing and encouraging as he shared his motivation, goals, vision, focus, and work ethic. I made a copy of it and gave it to my boys. I used that young man as a model.

Another of my strong beliefs from both personal experience and years in studying human behavior is that if people don't have goals and expectations, benchmarks and deadlines, often they will defer, avoid, and stall. My boys knew from the age of 13 or 14 that when they turned 18 and graduated from high school that, if they were not in college, they were out of the house. Period. This used to be an unstated expectation, something that was just understood in previous generations, something the young man, longing to be independent, anticipated. Over decades of subtle cultural decay, we have come to a low point where parents often have to push them out.

Today, many of our young men look for the path of least resistance, and weak fathers are all too willing to accommodate this apathetic attitude toward life. Just the other night at a dinner with friends, there was a single mom lamenting the plight of her 19-year-old son who was still living at home, racking up college debt at her expense, and then dropping out. He is now working a part-time job with no goals. The mom was torn between what she fundamentally knows is right – her son needs to take personal responsibility and get out – but also deals with the conflict of a mother who God wired naturally as a nurturer.

This isn't just the plight of single moms. Many two-parent (father and mother) homes deal with the same things. Remember the story of the eagle kicking the eaglet out of the nest? Sadly, in these situations, this is a failing of the father.

A butterfly, as you may know, has quite a fight to get out of its chrysalis. But the struggle is essential. The fight it goes through to break out of its chrysalis is essential for its survival; that struggle strengthens it, so that it can actually fly and survive when it emerges. Circumventing that process will cause the butterfly to die. When you make it easy on your son, instead of allowing him to experience the struggles and challenges of life, putting him intentionally in situations to learn and grow in a controlled environment, you cause him irreparable harm. You weaken him in ways you may not fully understand until you see it later in his life, when he has neither the wisdom to make good decisions, and/or doesn't have the inner fortitude to fight through challenges; when he folds on his marriage because it gets too difficult; when he quits his job because someone offends him; when he can't keep a job because he has no work ethic; when he gets a girl pregnant; and the list goes on.

Men, it is our responsibility; let's pick it up and run with it and secure a different future for our sons, one they and we can be proud of. How about the future promised in Jeremiah, chapter 29 and verse 11: *For I know the plans I have for you," says the Lord. "They are plans for good and not for disaster, to give you a future and a hope.*

CLOSING

In closing, as you are setting up your plan, remember to set a clear expectation for your son early on about his exit strategy. In business, you are taught to have an exit strategy. Be smart, and help yourself and your boy prepare for his exit. Additionally, having this conversation about his exit early and often begins to prepare your wife, his mom, for one of the most difficult moments of her life.

And just so you know, it will be hard for you, too! If you have developed the relationship with your boy(s), spent time and created eternal memories, if you have loved them passionately (albeit, not perfectly), you've been their coach and counselor, you've been their harshest critic and biggest fan, it will be glorious and gut wrenching all at the same time. It's time to get busy, create your plan, put it all together, and get started. Don't be intimidated by this process; just write it out, plan it out, and then make the commitment to execute! And remember:

"A year from now you'll wish you had started today."

– Robert Schuller

ABOUT THE AUTHOR

Allen Jones was born in Kirkland, WA, June 15, 1964. He is the oldest of three children; he has one brother and one sister. The family lived in various places when he was a child, as his father was in the Air Force. His family finally settled down in Federal Way, WA, where he graduated from Decatur High School in 1982.

He joined the Navy in 1982. While in the Navy, he visited many different countries and experienced different cultures: Africa, Singapore, Philippines, and Australia. He received his AA in Business Management while in the Navy, and married his wife, Donna. Allen was honorably discharged in 1990, with many accolades for his service. It was also during this time that Allen and Donna were divorced for the first time, and ultimately remarried.

A series of career changes followed. He was a Transportation Manager for a non-profit agency responsible for elderly and handicapped transport in eight counties in Washington state. He was the Service Manager for a Goodyear Auto Center. He was a salesman for a Toyota dealership, where he was repeatedly recognized over his four years there for both sales excellence and customer service. During these years, he and Donna had their two sons, Devan and Brendan, Allen became a born again Christian, and he and Donna divorced for the second time.

Allen changed careers, yet again, after he and Donna divorced. He was hired by a company to market personal development training to Direct Sales and Network Marketing companies. Here, he met his friend and future business partner. Together they started and led their business Diversified Learning Partners for 12 years. During this time, he and his business partner led more than 10,000 people through their development processes with such companies as Starbucks, Panera Bread, and Jack In The Box. It was here that Allen discovered his true gift – to equip people to experience positive change, in addition to his leadership and management gifts. It was also during this time that Donna became a born again Christian, they were remarried a third (and final) time, and they had their third child, daughter ClaraAnn.

Eventually, through God's guiding hand, and a transitional period in which the business was closed, Allen found himself in his current position as a staff pastor at Puyallup Foursquare Church. He has been an active member of the church for over a decade, served on the church council for four years, has now been an employee in vocational ministry for three years, and he is a licensed minister. It is here that all his life experiences coalesced into his calling.

There is nothing he enjoys more than helping and watching people grow and find true freedom to live a fulfilling life through and for God. His greatest joy, though, is found in working with fathers to equip their sons, and with young men who didn't get what they needed when they were boys, so they can change their legacy.

BIBLIOGRAPHY

Intelligent people are always ready to learn.
Their ears are open for knowledge.

– Solomon, Proverbs 18:15

What follows is more than just a traditional bibliography. I would personally characterize this list as essential reading material for you and your son's lives. They were for me. No doubt you will discover your own "gems" and you know men that have great titles to recommend that are not on this list. And there are books missing from this list that I have read that have influenced me as a father.

Although this is not a parenting book, parenting is your role, and this process cannot be separated out from parenting. As an imperfect father, I am much better today than I was ten years ago. In large part, I owe my growth and improvement to the knowledge I gained from the experience and wisdom of the following authors. I have personally read all these books. To them I owe a debt of gratitude.

God:
The Bible

James Dobson:
Bringing Up Boys, Tyndale House Publishers Inc, Wheaton, Ill, Copyright 2001
Strong Willed Child, Tyndale House Publishers Inc, Carol Stream, Ill, Copyright 2004
Dare to Discipline, Tyndale House Publishers Inc, Carol Stream, Ill, Copyright 1992
Parents Answer Book, Tyndale House Publishers Inc, Wheaton, Ill, Copyright 2003
Additionally, his daily radio broadcasts

Dennis & Barbara Rainey:
Parenting Today's Adolescent, Thomas Nelson Publishers, Nashville, TN, Copyright 1998
Passport2Purity, Family Life Publishing, Little Rock, AR, May 2012
Additionally his daily radio broadcasts

Gary Smalley & John Trent:
The Blessing, Pocket Books (Simon & Schuster), New York, NY, Copyright 1986

Gary Chapman & Ross Campbell:
The Five Love Languages of Children, Northfield Publishing, Chicago, IL, Copyright 2012

John Eldredge:
Wild At Heart, Thomas Nelson Publishing, Nashville, TN, Copyright 2002
The Way Of The Wild Heart, Thomas Nelson Publishing, Nashville, TN, Copyright 2006
Fathered By God, Thomas Nelson Publishing, Nashville, TN, Copyright 2009

Ron Luce:
Battle Cry for a Generation, Published by David C. Cook, Copyright June 2005,

John Maxwell
Becoming a Person of Influence, Published by Thomas Nelson, Inc, Copyright 1997

Dale Carnegie
How to Win Friends and Influence People, Published by Simon & Schuster, copyright Dale Carnegie 1936, renewed by Donna Dale Carnegie and Dorothy Carnegie 1981

Michael Popkin:
Active Parenting For Teens (workbook), Active Parenting Publishers Inc, Atlanta, GA, Copyright 2009

Michael Gurian:
The Good Son, published by Jeremy T. Tarcher/Putnam, copyright Michael Gurian 1999

Lee Strobel:
A Case for Christ, Zondervan Publishing, Copyright 1998

Stephen Arterburn, Fred Stoeker and Mike Yorkey:
Every Young Man's Battle, Published by Water Brook Press, Copyright 2002

Steve Farar:
Point Man, Multnomah Publishers Inc, Copyright 2003

Patrick Morley:
Man In The Mirror, Zondervan Publishing, Grand Rapids, MI, Copyright 2000

Stu Weber:
Tender Warrior, Multnomah Publishing, Copyright 1993

—

END NOTES

Introduction:
www.baldeagleinfo.com

Chapter 1:
[1]*The Good Son*, Michael Gurian, published by Jeremy T.
  Tarcher/Putnam, copyright Michael Gurian 1999

Chapter 3:
[1] *The Greatest Generation*, Tom Brokaw, Copyright 2004, Published by
  Random House
[2] J. Crew Executive Who Featured Son in Controversial Ad
  Reportedly Divorcing Husband for Woman, FoxNews.com,
  Published October 26, 2011
[3] PBS, Frontline, Merchants of Cool, A report on the creators &
  marketers of popular culture for teenagers, Published February,
  2001

Chapter 5:
[1] *A Case for Christ*, Author Lee Strobel, Copyright 1998 Zondervan
  Publishing

Chapter 7:
[1]*The Seven Habits of Highly Effective People*, Stephen Covey,
  Copyright 1989 and 2004 Stephen covey, Published by Free Press, a
  division of Simon & Schuster, Inc.

Chapter 8:
[1]Youth Risk Behavior Surveillance – USA, 2009, Surveillance
  Summaries, June 4, 2010
[2]*Battle Cry for a Generation*, Ron Luce, Copyright June 2005,Published
  by David C. Cook
[3]Plenty of Questions but no easy answers in wake of gang rape, Los
  Angeles Times, October 31, 2009

Chapter 8 (continued):
[4]*The Flipside of Feminism,* Phyllis Schlafley and Suzanne Venker, Copyright 2010, Published by WND books

Chapter 9:
[1]*Every Young Man's Battle,* Stephen Arterburn, Fred Stoeker and Mike Yorkey, Copyright 2002, Published by Water Brook Press

Chapter 10:
[1]Harvard Business Review, Decoding Steve Jobs, Trust the Art, Not the Artist, William C. Taylor (co-founder of Fast Company Magazine), June 23, 2009, HBR.ORG
[2]*How to Win Friends and Influence People,* Dale Carnegie, published by Simon & Schuster, copyright Dale Carnegie 1936, renewed by Donna Dale Carnegie and Dorothy Carnegie 1981
[3]*Becoming a Person of Influence,* John Maxwell, published by Thomas Nelson, Inc, Copyright 1997
[4]*Fierce Conversations,* Susan Scott, published by The Berkley Publishing Group, copyright Fierce Conversations, Inc. 2002

Chapter 11:
[1]*Financial Peace,* Dave Ramsey, published & copyright Dave Ramsey 1992
[2]*Financial Peace University,* Dave Ramsey, published by The Lampo Group, Inc, copyright the Lampo Group, Inc. 2008

Chapter 13:
[1]*Wild At Heart,* Thomas Nelson Publishing, Nashville, TN, Copyright 2002
[2]*The Way of the Wild Heart,* Thomas Nelson Publishing, Nashville, TN, Copyright 2006

Chapter 15:
[1]*The Knowing Doing Gap,* Jeffrey Pfeffer and Robert I. Sutton, published by Harvard Business School Publishing, copyright 2000 President and Fellows Harvard College